The Complete John Ploughman

John Ploughman's Talk
&
John Ploughman's Pictures

C. H. Spurgeon

© Christian Focus Publications

10 9 8 7 6 5 4 3 2 1

ISBN 1-84550-278-7
ISBN 978-1-84550-278-2

First published in the complete edition in 2007
in the
Christian Heritage imprint
by
Christian Focus Publications,
Geanies House, Fearn, Tain,
Ross-shire, IV20 1TW, Scotland
www.christianfocus.com

Cover design by Moose77.com
Printed and bound by CPD, Wales

Contents

John Ploughman's Talk;

or

Plain Advice for Plain People

by
C. H. Spurgeon

"What's rotten will rend."

Preface

In John Ploughman's Talk, I have tried to talk for ploughmen and common people. Hence refined taste and dainty words have been discarded for strong old proverbial expressions and homely phrases. I have aimed my blows at the vices of the many, and tried to inculcate those moral virtues without which men are degraded and miserable. Much that needs to be said to the toiling masses would not suit well the pulpit and the Sabbath; these lowly pages may teach thrift and industry all the days of the week, in the cottage and the workshop; and if some learn these lessons I shall not repent the adoption of the rustic style.

Ploughman is a name I may justly claim. Every minister has put his hand to the plough; it is his business to break up the fallow ground and cast in good seed. That I have written in a semi-humorous vein shall need no apology if thereby sound moral teaching wins a hearing from the million. There is no particular virtue in being seriously unreadable.

C. H. Spurgeon

1
To the Idle

It is of no more use to give advice to the idle than to pour water into a sieve; and as to improving them, one might as well try to fatten a greyhound. Yet, as The Old Book tells us to "cast our bread upon the waters," we will cast a hard crust or two upon these stagnant ponds; for there will be this comfort about it: if lazy fellows grow no better, we shall be none the worse for having warned them, for when we sow good sense, the basket gets none the emptier. We have a stiff bit of soil to plough when we chide with sluggards, and the crop will be of the smallest; but if none but good land were farmed, ploughmen would be out of work, so we'll put the plough into the furrow. Idle men are common enough, and grow without planting, but the quantity of wit among seven acres of them would never pay for raking: nothing is needed to prove this but their name and their character; if they were not fools they would not be idlers; and though Solomon says, "The sluggard is wiser in his own conceit than seven men that can render a reason," yet in the eyes of every one else his folly is as plain as the sun in the sky. If I hit hard while speaking to them, it is because I know they can bear it; for if I had them down on the floor of the old barn, I might thresh many a day before I could get them out of the straw, and even the steam thresher could not do it, it would kill them first; for laziness is in some people's bones and will show itself in their idle flesh, do what you will with them.

Well, then, first and foremost, it strikes me that lazy people ought to have a large looking-glass hung up, where they are bound to see themselves in it; for sure, if their eyes are at all like mine, they would never bear to look at themselves long or often. The ugliest sight in the world is one of those thorough-bred loafers, who would hardly hold up his basin if it were to rain porridge; and for certain would never hold up a bigger pot than he wanted filled for himself. Perhaps, if the shower should turn to beer, he might wake himself up a bit; but he would make up for it afterwards. This is the slothful man in the Proverbs, who "hideth his hand in his bosom; it grieveth him to bring it again to his mouth." I say that men the like of this ought to be served like the drones which the bees drive out of the hives. Every man ought to have patience and pity for poverty; but for laziness, a long whip or a turn at the treadmill might be better. This would be healthy physic for all sluggards; but there is no chance of some of them getting their full dose of this medicine, for they were born with silver spoons in their mouths, and, like spoons, they will scarce stir their own tea unless somebody lends them a hand. They are, as the old proverb says, "as lazy as Ludham's dog, that leaned his head against the wall to bark"; and, like lazy sheep, it is too much trouble for them to carry their own wool. If they could see themselves, it might by chance do them a world of good; but perhaps it would be too much trouble for them to open their eyes even if the glass were hung for them.

"Perhaps if the shower should turn to beer,
he might wake himself up a bit."

Everything in the world is of some use; but it would puzzle a doctor of divinity, or a philosopher, or the wisest owl in our steeple to tell the good of idleness: that seems to me to be an ill wind which blows nobody any good—a sort of mud which breeds no eels, a dirty ditch which would not feed a frog. Sift a sluggard grain by grain, and you'll find him all chaff. I have heard men say, "Better do nothing than do mischief," but I am not even sure of that: that saying glitters well, but I don't believe it's gold. I grudge laziness even that pinch of praise, I say it is bad and bad altogether; for look ye, a man doing mischief is a sparrow picking the corn—but a lazy man is a sparrow sitting on a nest full of eggs, which will all turn to sparrows before long and do a world of hurt. Don't tell me, I'm sure of it, that the rankest weeds on earth don't grow in the minds of those who are busy at wickedness but in foul corners of idle men's imaginations, where the devil can hide away unseen like an old serpent as he is. I don't like our boys to be in mischief, but I would sooner see them up to their necks in the mud in their larks ,than sauntering about with nothing to do. If the evil of doing nothing seems to be less today, you will find it out to be greater tomorrow; the devil is putting coals on the fire, and so the fire does not blaze; but depend upon it, it will be a bigger fire in the end. Idle people, you had need be your own trumpeters, for no one else can find any good in you to praise. I'd sooner see you through a telescope than anything else, for I suppose you would then be a long way off; but the biggest pair of spectacles in the parish could not see anything in you worth talking about. Moles, and rats, and weasels, there is something to be said for, though there's a pretty sight of them nailed up on our old barn, but as for you - well, you'll be of use in the grave and help to make a fat churchyard, but no better song can I sing in your favour than this verse, as the parish clerk said, "all of my own composing"—

> A good for nothing lazy lout,
> Wicked within and ragged without
> Who can bear to have him about?
> Turn him out! Turn him out!

"As vinegar to the teeth, and as smoke to the eyes," so is the sluggard to every man who is spending his sweat to earn an honest living, while these fellows let the grass grow up to their ankles, and stand cumbering the ground, as the Bible says.

A man who wastes his time and his strength in sloth offers himself to be a target for the devil, who is a wonderfully good rifleman and will riddle the idler with his shots: in other words, idle men tempt the devil to tempt them. He who plays when he should work has an evil spirit to be his playmate; and he who neither works nor plays is a workshop for Satan. If the devil catch a man idle, he will set him to work, find his tools, and before long pay him wages. Is not this where the drunkenness comes from which fills our towns and villages with misery? Idleness is the key of beggary and the root of all evil. Fellows have two stomachs for eating and drinking when they have no stomach for work. That little hole just under the nose swallows up in idle hours that money which should put clothes on the children's backs and bread on the cottage table. We have God's word

13

for it, that "the drunkard and the glutton shall come to poverty"; and to show the connection between them, it is said in the same verse, "and drowsiness shall clothe a man with rags." I know it as well as I know that moss grows on old thatch, that drunken, loose habits grow out of lazy hours. I like leisure when I can get it, but that's quite another thing; that's cheese and the other is chalk: idle folks never know what leisure means; they are always in a hurry and a mess, and by neglecting to work in the proper time, they always have a lot to do. Lolling about hour after hour, with nothing to do, is just making holes in the hedge to let the pigs through; and they will come through, and no mistake, and the rooting they will do nobody knows but those who have to look after the garden. The Lord Jesus tells us Himself that when men slept the enemy sowed the tares; and that hits the nail on the head, for it is by the door of sluggishness that evil enters the heart more often it seems to me than by any other. Our old minister used to say, "A sluggard is fine raw material for the devil; he can make anything he likes out of him from a thief right up to a murderer." I'm not the only one that condemns the idle, for once when I was going to give our minister a pretty long list of the sins of one of our people that he was asking after, I began with "he's dreadfully lazy." "That's enough," said the old gentleman, "all sorts of sins are in that one, that's the sign by which to know a full-fledged sinner."

My advice to my boys has been, get out of the sluggard's way, or you may catch his disease and never get rid of it. I am always afraid of their learning the ways of the idle and am very watchful to nip anything of that sort in the bud; for you know it is best to kill the lion while it is a cub. Sure enough our children have all our evil nature about them, for you can see it growing of itself like weeds in a garden. Who can bring a clean thing out of the unclean? A wild goose never lays a tame egg. Our boys will be off to the green with the ne'er-do-wells unless we make it greener still at home for them, and train them up to hate the company of the slothful. Never let them go to the "Rose and Crown"; let them learn to earn a crown while they are young and grow the roses in their father's garden at home. Bring them up bees and they will not be drones.

There is much talk about bad masters and mistresses nowadays, and I dare say that there is a good deal in it, for there's bad of all sorts now as there always was; another time, if I am allowed, I will have a say about that matter; but I am sure there is plenty of room for complaint against some among the working people too, especially upon this matter of slothfulness. You know we are obliged to plough with such cattle as we have found for us; but when I am set to work with some men, I'd as soon drive a team of snails, or go out rabbit hunting with a dead ferret. Why, you might sooner get blood out of a gatepost or juice out of a cork than work out of some of them; and yet they are always talking about their right; I wish they would give an eye to their own wrongs, and not lean on the plough-handles. Lazy lie-a-beds are not working men at all, any more than pigs are bullocks, or thistles apple trees. All are not hunters that wear red coats, and all are not working men who call themselves so. I wonder sometimes that some of our employers keep so many cats who catch no mice. I would as soon drop my halfpence down a well as pay some people for pretending to work who only fidget you and make your flesh crawl to see them all day creeping over a cabbage leaf. Live and let live, say I, but I don't include sluggards in that license; for they who will not work, neither let them eat.

Here, perhaps, is the proper place to say that some of the higher classes, as they are called, set a shamefully bad example in this respect: our great folks are some of them quite as lazy as they are rich, and often more so; the big dormice sleep as long and as sound as the little ones. Many a parson buys or hires a sermon so that he may save himself the trouble of thinking. Is not this abominable laziness? They sneer at the ranters; but there is not a ranter in the kingdom that would not be ashamed to stand up and read somebody else's sermon as if it were his own. Many of our squires have nothing to do but to part their hair in the middle; and many of the London grandees, ladies and gentlemen both alike, as I am told, have no better work than killing time. Now, they say the higher a monkey climbs, the more his tail is seen; and so, the greater these people are, the more their idleness is noticed, and the more they ought to be ashamed of it. I don't say they ought to plough, but I do say that they ought to do something for the state besides being like the caterpillars on the cabbage, eating up the good things; or like the butterflies, showing themselves off but making no honey. I cannot be angry with these people somehow, for I pity them when I think of the stupid rules of fashion which they are forced to mind, and the vanity in which they weary out their days. I'd sooner by half

bend my back double with hard work, than be a jack-a-
dandy, with nothing to do but to look in the glass and
see in it a fellow who never put a single potato into the
nation's pot, but took a good many out. Let me drop on
these Surrey hills, worn out like my master's old brown
mare, sooner than eat bread and cheese, and never earn
it; better die an honourable death than live a good-for-
nothing's life. Better to get into my coffin than be dead
and alive, a man whose life is a blank.

However, it is not much ease that lazy people get by
all their scheming, for they always take the most pains
in the end; they will not mend the thatch, and so they
have to build a new cottage; they will not put the horse
in the cart, and so have to drag it themselves. If they were
wise, they would do their work well, so as to save doing it
twice; and tug hard while they are in harness, so as to get
the work out of the way. My advice is, if you don't like
hard work, just pitch into it, settle it off, and have your
turn at rest.

I wish all religious people would take this matter under
their consideration; for some professors are amazingly
lazy, and make sad work for the tongues of the wicked.
I think a godly ploughmen ought to be the best man in
the field, and let no team beat him. When we are at work,
we ought to be at it, and not stop the plough to talk,
even though the talk may be about religion; for then we
not only rob our employers of our own time, but of the
time of the horses, too. I used to hear people say, "Never
stop the plough to catch a mouse," and it's quite as silly
to stop for idle chat; besides, the man who loiters when
the master is away is an eye-server, which, I take it, is the

very opposite of a Christian. If some of the members at our meeting were a little more spry with their arms and legs when they are at labour and a little quieter with their tongues, they would say more for religion than they now do. The world says the greatest rogue is the pious rogue, and I'm sorry to say one of the greatest sluggards I know of is a professing man of the "Mr. Talkative" kind. His garden is so overgrown with weeds that I feel often half a mind to weed it for him, to save our meeting the shame which he brings upon it: if he were a young lad, I'd talk to him about it and try to teach him better, but who can be a school-master to a child sixty years old? He is a regular thorn to our good minister, who is quite grieved about it and sometimes says he will go somewhere else because he cannot bear such conduct; but I tell him that wherever a man lives he is sure to have one thorn bush near his door, and it is a mercy if there are not two. However, I do wish that all Christians would be industrious, for religion never was destined to make us idle. Jesus was a great worker, and his disciples must not be afraid of hard work.

As to serving the Lord with cold hearts and drowsy souls, there has been too much of it, and it causes religion to wither. Men ride stags when they hunt for gain, andsnails when they are on the road to heaven. Preachers go on see-sawing, droning, and prosing; and the people fall to yawning and folding their arms, and then say that God is withholding the blessing. Every sluggard, when he finds himself enlisted in the ragged regiment, blames his luck, and some churches have learned the same wicked trick. I believe that when Paul plants and Apollos waters,

God gives the increase, and I have no patience with those who throw the blame on God when it belongs to themselves.

Now I have come to the end of my tether. I am afraid I have been watering a dead snake, but I have done my best, and a king can do no more. An ant can never make honey if it works its heart out, and I shall never put my thoughts so prettily together as some do, book-fashion; but truth is truth, even when dressed in homespun, and so there is an end of my rigmarole.

2
On Religious Grumblers

When a man has a particularly empty head, he generally sets up for a great judge, especially in religion. None so wise as the man who knows nothing. His ignorance is the mother of his impudence and the nurse of his obstinacy; and though he does not know B from a bull's foot, he settles matters as if all wisdom were at his fingers' ends—the Pope himself is not more infallible. Hear him talk after he has been at a meeting and heard a sermon, and you will know how to pull a good man to pieces if you never knew it before. He sees faults where there are none; and if there be a few things amiss, he makes every mouse into an elephant. Although you might put all his wit into an egg-shell, he weighs the sermon in the balances of his conceit with all the airs of a born-and-bred Solomon, and if it be up to his standard, he lays on his praise with a trowel; but if it be not to his taste, he growls and barks and snaps at it like a dog at a hedgehog.

Wise men in this world are like trees in a hedge; there is only here and there one, and when these rare men talk together upon a discourse, it is good for the ears to hear them; but the bragging wiseacres I am speaking of are vainly puffed up by their fleshly minds, and their quibbling is as senseless as the cackle of geese on a common. Nothing comes out of a sack but what was in it; and as their bag is empty they shake nothing but wind out of it. It is very likely that neither ministers nor their sermons are perfect—the best garden may have a few weeds in it, the cleanest corn may have some chaff—but cavillers cavil at anything or nothing, and find fault for the sake of showing off their deep knowledge; sooner than let their tongues have a holiday they would complain that the grass is not a nice shade of blue, and say that the sky would have looked neater if it had been whitewashed.

One tribe of these Ishmaelites is made up of high-flying ignoramuses who are very mighty about the doctrine of a sermon – here they are as decisive as sledge-hammers and as certain as death. He who knows nothing is confident in everything; hence they are bullheaded beyond measure. Every clock, and even the sundial, must be set according to their watches and the slightest difference from their opinion proves a man to be rotten at heart. Venture to argue with them, and their little pots boil over in quick style; ask them for reason, and you might as well go to a sand pit for sugar. They have bottled up the sea of truth, and carry it in their waistcoat pockets; they have measured heaven's line of grace and have tied a knot in a string at the exact length of electing love; and as for the things which angels long to know, they have seen them all as boys see sights in a peep-show at our fair. Having sold their modesty and become wiser than their teachers, they ride a very high horse and jump over all five-barred gates of Bible texts which teach doctrines contrary to their notions. When this mischief happens to good men, it is a great pity for such sweet pots of ointment to be spoiled by flies, yet one learns to bear with them just as I do with old Violet, for he is a rare horse, though he does set his ears back and throw out his legs at times. But there is a bragging lot about, who are all sting and no honey, all whip and no hay, all grunt and no bacon. These do nothing but rail from morning to night at all who cannot see through their spectacles. If they would but mix up a handful of good living with all their bushels of bounce, it would be more bearable; but no, they don't care for such legality; men so sound as they are can't be expected to be good at anything else; they are the heavenly watchdogs to guard the house of the Lord from those thieves and robbers who don't preach sound doctrine, and if they do worry the sheep, or steal a rabbit or two by the sly, who would have the heart to blame them? The Lord's *dear* people, as they call themselves, have enough to do to keep their doctrine sound; and if their manners are cracked, who can wonder! No man can see to everything at once. These are the moles that want catching in many of our pastures, not for their own sakes, for there is not a sweet mouthful in them, but for the sake of the meadows which they spoil. I would not find half a fault with their doctrine if it were not for their spirit, but vinegar is sweet next to it, and crabs are figs in comparison. It must be very high doctrine that is too high for me, but I must have high experience and high practice with it, or it turns my stomach. However, I have said my say, and must leave the subject, or somebody will ask me, "what have you to do with Bradshaw's windmill?"

Sometimes it is the way the preacher speaks which is hauled over the coals, and here again is a fine field for fault hunting, for every bean has its black, and every man has his failing. I never knew a good horse which had not some odd habit or other, and I never yet saw a minister worth his salt who had not some crotchet or oddity: now, these are the bits of cheese which cavillers smell out and nibble at; this man is too slow, and another too fast, the first is too flowery, and the second is too dull. Dear me, if all God's creatures were judged in this way, we should wring the dove's neck for being too tame, shoot the robins for eating spiders, kill the cows for swinging their tails and the hens for not giving us milk. When a man wants to beat a dog, he can soon find a stick; and at this rate, any fool may have something to say against the best minister in England.

As to a preacher's manner, if there be but plain speaking, none should cavil at it because it wants polish, for if a thing is good and earnestly spoken, it cannot sound much amiss. No man should use bad language in the pulpit—and all language is bad which common people cannot make head or tail of—but godly, sober, decent, plain words none should carp at. A countryman is as warm in fustian as a king in velvet, and a truth is as comfortable in homely words as in fine speech. As to the way of dishing up the meat, hungry men leave that to the cook, only let the meat be sweet and substantial. If hearers were better , sermons would be better. When men say they can't hear, I recommend them to buy a horn and remember the old saying, "There's none so deaf as those who will not hear." When young speakers get downhearted because of hard, unkind remarks, I generally tell them of the old man and his boy and his ass, and what came of trying to please everybody. No piper ever suited all ears. Where whims and fancies sit in the seat of judgment, a man's opinion is only so much wind, therefore take no more notice of it than of the wind whistling through a keyhole.

I have heard men find fault with a discourse for what was not in it; no matter how well the subject in hand was brought out, there was another subject about which nothing was said, and so all was wrong; which is as reasonable as finding fault with my ploughing because it does not dibble the holes for the beans, or abusing a good corn field because there are no turnips in it. Does any man look for every truth in one sermon? As well look for every dish at one meal, and rail at a joint of beef because there are neither bacon, nor veal, nor green peas, nor parsnips on the table. Suppose a sermon is not full of comfort to the saint; yet if it warn the sinner, shall we despise it? A handsaw would be a poor tool to shave with, shall we therefore throw it away? Where is the use of always trying to hunt out faults? I hate to see a man with a fine nose smelling about for things to rail at like a rat-catcher's dog sniffing at rat holes. By all means let us cut down error, root and branch, but do let us save our billhooks till there are brambles to chop, and not fall foul of our own mercies. Judging preachers is a poor trade, for it pays neither party concerned in it. At a ploughing match they do give a prize to the best of us; but these judges of preaching are precious slow to give anything even to those whom they profess to think so much of.

They pay in praise, but give no pudding. They get the gospel for nothing, and if they do not grumble, think that they have made an abundant return.

Everybody thinks himself a judge of a sermon, but nine out of ten might as well pretend to weigh the moon. I believe that at bottom, most people think it an uncommonly easy thing to preach, and that they could do it amazingly well themselves. Every donkey thinks itself worthy to stand with the king's horses; every girl thinks she could keep house better than her mother; but thoughts are not facts, for the sprat thought itself a herring, yet the fisherman knew better. I dare say those who can whistle fancy that they can plough; but there's more than whistling in a good ploughman, and so let me tell you there's more in good preaching than taking a text and saying, firstly, secondly, and thirdly. I try my hand at preaching myself, and in my poor way I find it no very easy thing to give the folks something worth hearing; and if the fine critics, who reckon us up on their thumbs, would but try their own hands at it, they might be a little more quiet. Dogs, however, always will bark, and what is worse, some of them will bite too; but let decent people do all they can, if not to muzzle them, yet to prevent them doing any great mischief. It is a dreadful thing to see a happy family of Christians broken up by talkative fault-finders, and all about nothing, or less than nothing. Small is the edge of the wedge, but when the devil handles the beetle, churches are soon split to pieces, and men wonder why.

The fact is, the worst wheel of the cart creaks most, and one fool makes many, and thus many a congregation is set at ears with a good and faithful minister, who would have been a lasting blessing to them if they had not chased away their best friend. Those who are at the bottom of the mischief have generally no part or lot in the matter of true godliness, but, like sparrows, fight over corn which is not their own, and, like jackdaws, pull to pieces what they never helped to build. From mad dogs, and grumbling professors, may we all be delivered, and may we never take the complaint from either of them.

3
On the Preacher's Appearance

A good horse cannot be a bad colour, and a really good preacher can wear what he likes, and none will care much about it; but though you cannot know wine by the barrel, a good appearance is a letter of recommendation even to a ploughman. Wise men neither fall into love nor take a dislike at first sight, but still the first impression is always a great thing even with them; and as to those weaker brethren who are not wise, a good appearance is half the battle. What is a good appearance? Well, it's not being pompous and starchy, and making one's self high and mighty among the people, for proud looks lose hearts, and gentle words win them. It's not wearing fine clothes either, for foppish dress usually means a foul house within, and the doorstep without fresh whitened; such dressing tells the world that the outside is the best part of the puppet.

When a man is proud as a peacock, all strut and show, he needs converting himself before he sets up to preach to others. The preacher who measures himself by his looking-glass, may please a few silly girls, but neither God nor man will long put up with him. The man who owes his greatness to his tailor will find that needle and thread cannot long hold a fool in the pulpit. A gentleman should have more in his pocket than on his back, and a minister should have more in his inner man than on his outer man. I would say, if I might, to young ministers, do not preach in gloves, for cats in mittens catch no mice; don't curl and oil your hair like dandies, for nobody cares to hear a peacock's voice; don't have your own pretty self in your mind at all, or nobody else will mind you. Away with gold rings, and chains, and jewellery; why should the pulpit become a goldsmith's shop? Forever away with surplices and gowns and all those nursery doll dresses men should put away childish things. A cross on the back is the sign of a devil in the heart; those who do as Rome does should go to Rome and show their colors. If the priests of Rome suppose that they get the respect of honest men by their fine ornamental dresses, they are much mistaken, for it is commonly said, "Fine feathers make fine birds," and "An ape is never so like an ape as when he wears a Popish cape."

I would say, let fools wear fools' caps and fools' dresses, but men who make no claim to be fools should not put on fools' clothes. None but a very silly sheep would wear wolf's clothing. It is a singular taste which makes honest men covet the rag of thieves. Besides, where's the good of such finery? Except a duck in pattens, no creature looks more stupid than a Dissenting preacher in a gown which is of no manner of use to him. I could laugh till I held my sides when I see our doctors in gowns and bands, puffed out with their silks, and touched up with their little bibs, for they put me so much in mind of our old turkey when his temper is up, and he swells to his biggest. They must be weak folks indeed who want a man to dress like a woman before they can enjoy his sermon, and he who cannot preach without such milliner's tawdry finery may be a man among geese, but he is a goose among men.

At the same time, the preacher should endeavour, according to his means, to dress himself respectably; and, as to neatness, he should be without spot, for kings should not have dirty footmen to wait at their table, and they who teach godliness should practise cleanliness. I should like white neckties better *if they were always white*, but dirty brown is neither here nor there. From a slovenly, smoking, snuff-taking, beer-drinking preacher may the church be delivered. Some that I meet with may, perhaps, have very good manners, but they did not happen to have them about them at the time: like the Dutch captain with his anchors, they had left them at home; this should never be the case, for, if there be a well-behaved man in the parish, it should be the minister.

A worn coat is no discredit, but the poorest may be neat, and men should be scholars rather than teachers till they are so. You cannot judge a horse by his harness; but a modest, gentlemanly appearance, in which the dress is just such as nobody could make a remark upon, seems to me to be the right sort of thing. This little bit of my mind is meant to warn you young striplings who have just started in the ministry, and if any of you get cross over it, I shall tell you that sore horses cannot bear to be combed, and again, "those whom the cap fits must wear it." John Ploughman, you will say, had better mend his own smock and let the parsons alone; but I take leave to look about me and speak my mind, for a cat may look at a king, and a fool may give wise men good advice.

If I speak too plainly, please remember that an old dog cannot alter his way of barking, and he who has long been used to plough a straight furrow, is very apt to speak in the same straightforward manner.

4
On Good Nature and Firmness

Do not be all sugar, or the world will suck you down; but do not be all vinegar or the world will spit you out. There is a medium in all things, only blockheads go to extremes. We need not be all rock or all sand, all iron or all wax. We should neither fawn upon everybody like silly lapdogs, nor fly at all persons like surly mastiffs. Blacks and whites go together to make up a world, and hence on the point of temper, we have all sorts of people to deal with. Some are as easy as an old shoe, but they are hardly ever worth more than the other one of the pair; and others take fire as fast as tinder at the smallest offence and are as dangerous as gunpowder. To have a fellow going about the farm as cross with everybody as a bear with a sore head, with a temper as sour as spoiled milk and as sharp as a razor, looking as surly as a butcher's dog, is a great nuisance; and yet there may be some good points about the man, so that he may be a man for all that, but poor soft Tommy, as green as grass, and as ready to bend as a willow, is nobody's money and everybody's scorn. A man must have a backbone, or how is he to hold his head up? But that backbone must bend, or he will knock his brow against the beam.

There is a time to do as others wish, and a time to refuse. We make ourselves asses, then everybody will ride us, but if we would be respected, we must be our own masters and not let others saddle us as they think fit. If we try to please everybody, we shall be like a toad under a harrow, and never have peace; and if we play lackey to all our neighbours, whether good or bad, we shall be thanked by no one, for we shall soon do as much harm as good. He that makes himself a sheep will find that the wolves are not all dead. He who lies on the ground must expect to be trodden on. He who makes himself a mouse, the cats will eat him. If you let your neighbours put the calf on your shoulder they will soon clap on the cow. We are to please our neighbour for his good to edification, but this is quite another matter.

There are old foxes about whose mouths are always watering for young geese, and if they can coax them to do just what they wish, they soon make their market out of them. What a jolly good fellow you will be called if you will make yourself a hack for your friends, and what a Benjamin's mess will they soon bring you into! Out of that mess you will have to get all alone, for your friends will be sure to say to you, "Good-bye, basket, I've carried all my apples" or they will give you their good wishes and nothing more, and you will find out that fair words won't feed a cat, nor butter your bread, nor fill your pocket. Those who make so very much of you either mean to cheat you, or else are in need of you: when they have sucked the orange they will throw the peel away. Be wise, then, and look before you leap, lest a friend's advice should do you more mischief than an enemy's slander.

"The simple believeth every word; but the prudent man looketh well to his going." Go with your neighbour as far as good conscience will go with you, but part company where the shoe of conscience begins to pinch your foot. Begin with your friend as you mean to go on, and let him know very early that you are not a man made of putty, but one who has a judgment of his own and means to use it. Pull up the moment you find you are out of the road, and take the nearest way back at once. The way to avoid great faults is to beware of small ones, therefore, pull up in time if you would not be dragged into the ditch by your friend. Better offend your acquaintance than lose your character and hazard your soul. Don't be ashamed to walk down Turnagain Lane. Never mind being called a turncoat when you turn from bad courses: better to turn in time than to burn in eternity. Do not be persuaded to ruin yourself—it is buying gold too dear to throw oneself away to please our company. Put your foot down where you mean to stand, and let no man move you from the right. Learn to say, "No," and it will be of more use to you than to be able to read Latin.

A friend to everybody is often a friend to nobody; or else in his simplicity, he robs his family to help strangers and becomes brother to a beggar. There is wisdom in generosity, as in everything else, and some had need go to school to learn it. A kind-hearted soul may be very cruel to his own children, while he takes the bread out of their mouths to give to those who call him a generous fellow, but laugh at his folly. Very often he that his money lends loses both his gold and his friends, and he who is surety is never sure. Take John Ploughman's advice, and never be security for more than you are quite willing to lose. Remember the word of God says, "He that is surety for a stranger shall smart for it: and he that hateth suretyship is sure."

When we are injured, we are bound as Christians to bear it without malice; but we are not to pretend that we do not feel it, for this will but encourage our enemies to kick us again. He who is cheated twice by the same man is half as bad as the rogue; and it is very much so in other injuries—unless we claim our rights, we are ourselves to blame if we do not get them. Paul was willing to bear stripes for his Master's sake, but he did not forget to tell the magistrates that he was a Roman; and when those gentlemen wished to put him out of prison privately, he said, "Nay, verily, let them come themselves and fetch us out". A Christian is the gentlest of men, but then he is a man.

A good many people don't need to be told this, for they are up in a moment if they think anybody is likely to ill treat them; long before they know whether it is a thief in the farmyard, or the old mare got loose, they up with the window and fire off the old blunderbuss. Dangerous neighbours these; a man might as well make a seat out of a bull's forehead, as expect to find comfort in their neighbourhood. Make no friendship with an angry man, and with a furious man thou shalt not go. "He that is slow to wrath is of great understanding; but he that is hasty of spirit exalteth folly." "Seest thou a man that is hasty in his words, there is more hope of a fool than of him."

In my day I have seen a few downright obstinate men, whom neither sense nor reason could alter. There's a queer chap in our village who keeps a bulldog, and he tells me that when the creature once gives a bite at anything, he never lets go again, and if you want to get it out of his mouth, you must cut his head off; that's the sort of man that has fretted me many a time and almost made me mad. You might sooner argue a pitchfork into a threshing machine, or persuade a brickbat to turn into marble, than get the fellow to hear common sense. Getting spots out of leopards is nothing at all compared with trying to lead a downright obstinate man. Right or wrong, you might as easily make a hill walk to London, as turn him when his mind is made up. When a man is right, this sticking to his text is a grand thing; our minister says, "it is the stuff that martyrs are made of;", but when an ignorant, wrong-headed fellow gets this hard grit into him, he makes martyrs of those who have to put up with him. Old Master Pighead swore he would drive a nail into an oak board with his fist, and so lamed his hand for life; he could not sell his corn at his own price, and so he let the rats eat up the ricks. You cannot ride by his fields without noticing his obstinacy, for he vows, "He won't have none of these 'ere newfangled notions," and so he grows the worst crops in the parish; and worst of all, his daughter went among the Methodists, and, in a towering rage, he turned her out of doors; and though I believe he is very sorry for it, he will not yield an inch, but stands to it that he will never speak to her so long as he lives, and meanwhile the dear girl is dying through his unkindness. Rash vows are much better broken than kept. He who never changes, never mends; he who never yields, never conquers.

With children, we must mix gentleness with firmness; they must not always have their own way, but they must

"Old Master Pighead swore he would drive a nail into an oak board with his fist, and so lamed his hand for life."

not always be thwarted. Give to a pig when it grunts, and to a child when it cries, and you will have a fine pig and a spoiled child. A man who is learning to play on a trumpet, and a petted child, are two very disagreeable companions even as next-door neighbours; but unless we look well to it, our children will be a nuisance to others and a torment to ourselves. "The rod and reproof give wisdom; but a child left to himself bringeth his mother to shame." If we never have headaches through rebuking our little children, we shall have plenty of heartaches when they grow up. Strict truthfulness must rule all our dealings with the young; our yea must be yea, and our nay nay," and that always. Never promise a child and then fail to perform, whether you promise him a bun or a beating. Be obeyed at all costs, disobedient children are unhappy children; for their own sakes, make them mind you. If you yield up your authority once, you will hardly ever get it again, for he who says A, must say B, and so on. We must not provoke our children to anger, lest they be discouraged, but we must rule our household in the fear of the Lord, and in so doing may expect a blessing.

Since John Ploughman has taken to writing, he has had a fine chance of showing his firmness and his gentleness too, for he has received bushels of advice for which he begs to present his compliments, as the squire's lady says, and he does not mind either returning the advice or some of his own instead, by way of showing his gratitude; for he is sure it is very kind of so many people to tell him so many different ways in which he might make an idiot of himself. He means to glean as many good hints as he can from the acres of his friends' stubble; and while sticking to his own style, because it suits his hand, he will touch himself up a bit if he can. Perhaps if the minister will lend him Cowper or Milton, he may even stick a sprig of poetry into his nosegay, and come out as fine as the flowers in May; but he cannot promise, for the harvest is just on and reaping leaves no time for rhyming. The worst of it is, the kind friends who are setting John to rights, contradict one another: one says it's very poor stuff, and all in an assumed name, for the style is not rough enough for a ploughman; and another says the matter is very well, but really the expressions are so coarse, he wonders the editor puts it in the magazine. John means to pay his advisers all the attention which they deserve, and as some of the mice have been bold enough to make a nest in the cat's ear, he means to be after them and write a paper upon giving advice gratis, in which they will be likely to get a flea in their ear in return for their instructions.

5

On Patience

Patience is better than wisdom: an ounce of patience is worth a pound of brains. All men praise patience, but few enough can practise it; it is a medicine which is good for all diseases and therefore every old woman recommends it: but it is not every garden that grows the herbs to make it with. When one's flesh and bones are full of aches and pains, it is as natural for us to murmur as for a horse to shake his head when the flies tease him, or a wheel to rattle when a spoke is loose; but nature should not be the rule with Christians, or what is their religion worth?

If a soldier fights no better than a ploughboy, off with his red coat. We expect more fruit from an apple tree than from a thorn, and we have a right to do so. The disciples of a patient Saviour should be patient themselves. Grin and bear it is the old-fashioned advice, but sing and bear it is a great deal better. After all, we get very few cuts of the whip considering what bad cattle we are; and when we do smart a little, it is soon over. Pain past is pleasure, and experience comes by it. We ought not to be afraid of going down into Egypt when we know we shall come out of it with jewels of silver and gold.

Impatient people water their miseries and plough up their comforts; sorrows are visitors that come without invitation, but complaining minds send a wagon to bring their troubles home in. Many people are born crying, live complaining, and die disappointed; they chew the bitter pill which they would not even know to be bitter if they had the sense to swallow it whole in a cup of patience and water. They think every other man's burden to be light, and their own feathers to be heavy as lead; they are hardly done by in their own opinion; no one's toes are so often trodden on by the black ox as theirs; the snow falls thickest round their door, and the hail rattles hardest on their windows; and yet, if the truth were known, it is their fancy rather than their fate which makes things go so hard with them. Many would be well off if they could but think so. A little sprig of the herb called content put into the poorest soup will make it taste as rich as the Lord Mayor's turtle. John Ploughman grows the plant in his garden, but the late hard winter nipped it terribly, so that he cannot afford to give his neighbours a slip of it; they had better follow Matthew 25:9, and go to those who sell and buy for themselves. Grace is a good soil to grow it in, but it wants watering from the fountain of mercy.

To be poor is not always pleasant, but worse things than that happen at sea. Small shoes are apt to pinch, but not if you have a small foot: if we have little means it will be well to have little desires. Poverty is no shame, but being discontented with it is. In some things the poor are better off than the rich; for if a poor man has to seek meat for his stomach, he is more likely to get what he is after, than the rich man who seeks a stomach for his meat. A poor man's table is soon spread, and his labour spares his buying sauce.

The best doctors are Dr. Diet, Dr. Quiet, and Dr. Merryman, and many a godly ploughman has all these gentlemen to wait upon him. Plenty makes dainty, but hunger finds no fault with the cook. Hard work brings health, and an ounce of health is worth a sack of diamonds. It is not how much we have, but how much we enjoy that makes happiness. There is more sweet in a spoonful of sugar than in a cask of vinegar. It is not the quantity of our goods, but the blessing of God on what we have that makes us truly rich. The parings of a pippin are better than a whole crab; a dinner of herbs with peace is better than a stalled ox and contention therewith. "Better is little with the fear of the Lord than great treasure and trouble therewith." A little wood will heat my little oven, why, then, should I murmur because all the woods are not mine?

When troubles come it is of no use to fly in the face of God by hard thoughts of providence: that is kicking against the pricks and hurting your feet. The trees bow in the wind, and so must we. Every time the sheep bleats it loses a mouthful, and every time we complain, we miss a blessing. Grumbling is a bad trade and yields no profit, but patience has a golden hand. Our evils will soon be over. After rain comes clear shining; black crows have wings; every winter turns to spring; every night breaks into morning.

> Blow the wind never so fast,
> It will lower at last.

If one door should be shut, God will open another; if the peas do not yield well, the beans may; if one hen leaves her eggs, another will bring out all her brood; there's a bright side to all things, and a good God everywhere. Somewhere or other in the worst flood of trouble, there always is a dry spot for contentment to get its foot on, and if there were not, it would learn to swim.

Friends, let us take to patience and water gruel, as the old folks used to tell us, rather than catch the miserables and give others the disease by wickedly finding fault with God. The best remedy for affliction is submitting to providence. What can't be cured must be endured. If we cannot get bacon, let us bless God that there are still some cabbages in the garden. Must is a hard nut to crack, but it has a sweet kernel. "All things work together for good to them that love God." Whatever falls from the skies is, sooner or later, good for the land: whatever comes to us from God is worth having, even though it be a rod. We cannot by nature like trouble any more than a mouse can fall in love with a cat, and yet Paul by grace came to glory in tribulations also. Losses and crosses are heavy to bear, but when our hearts are right with God, it is wonderful how easy the yoke becomes. We must needs go to glory by the way of Weeping Cross; and as we were never promised that we should ride to heaven in a feather bed, we must not be disappointed when we see the road to be rough, as our fathers found it before us. All's well that ends well; and, therefore, let us plough the heaviest soil with our eye on the sheaves of harvest, and learn to sing at our labour while others murmur.

6
On Gossips

In Walton church, in our county, there is a brank, or scold's bridle, which was used in years gone by to keep women's tongues from troubling their husbands and their neighbours. They did queer things in those good old times. Was this bridle a proof of what our parson calls the wisdom of our ancestors, or was it a bit of needless cruelty?

"It is nothing—only a woman drowning," is a wicked and spiteful old saying, which, like the bridle, came out of the common notion that women do a world of mischief with their tongues. Is it so or not? John Ploughman will leave somebody else to answer, for he owns that he cannot keep a secret himself, and likes a dish of chat as well as anybody; only John does not care for cracking people's characters, and hates the slander which is so sweet to some people's teeth. John puts the question to wiser men than himself: Are women much worse than men in this business? They say that silence is a fine jewel for a woman, but it is very little worn. Is it so? Is it true that a woman only conceals what she does not know? Are women's tongues like lambs' tails, always wagging? They say foxes are all tail, and women all tongue. Is this false or

not? Was that old prayer a needful one —"From big guns
and women's tongues deliver us?" John has a right good
and quiet wife of his own, whose voice is so sweet that
he cannot hear it too often, and, therefore, is not a fair
judge; but he is half afraid that some other women would
sooner preach than pray, and would not require strong tea
to set their clappers going; but still, what is sauce for the
goose is sauce for the gander, and some men are quite as
bad blabs as the women.

What a pity that there is not a tax upon words: what
an income the Queen would get from it; but, alas! talking
pays no toll. And if lies paid double, the government
might pay off the National Debt; but who could collect
the money? Common fame is a common liar. Hearsay is
half lies. A tale never loses in the telling. As a snowball
grows by rolling, so does a story. They who talk much lie
much. If men only said what was true, what a peaceable
world we should see. Silence seldom makes mischief; but
talking is a plague to the parish. Silence is wisdom; and,
by this rule, wise men and wise women are scarce. Still
waters are the deepest; but the shallowest brooks brawl
the most; this shows how plentiful fools must be. An
open mouth shows an empty head. If the chest had gold or
silver in it, it would not always stand wide open. Talking
comes by nature, but it needs a good deal of training to
learn to be quiet; yet regard for truth should put a bit
into every honest man's mouth, and a bridle upon every
good woman's tongue.

If we must talk, at least let us be free from slander, let
us not blister our tongues with backbiting. Slander may
be sport to talebearers, but it is death to those whom

they abuse. We can commit murder with the tongue as well as with the hand. The worst evil you can do a man is to injure his character, as the Quaker said to his dog, "I'll not beat thee, nor abuse thee, but I'll give thee an ill name." All are not thieves that dogs bark at, but they are generally treated as if they were; for the world for the most part believe that where there is smoke there is fire, and what everybody says must be true. Let us then be careful that we do not hurt our neighbour in so tender a point as his character, for it is hard to get dirt off if it is once thrown on; and when a man is once in people's bad books, he is hardly ever quite out of them. If we would be sure not to speak amiss, it might be as well to speak as little as possible; for if all men's sins were divided into two bundles, half of them would be sins of the tongue. "If any man offend not in word, the same is a perfect man, and able also to bridle the whole body."

Gossips of both genders, give up the shameful trade of talebearing; don't be the devil's bellows any longer to blow up the fire of strife. Leave off setting people by the ears. If you do not cut a bit off your tongues, at least season them with the salt of grace. Praise God more and blame neighbours less. Any goose can cackle, any fly can find out a sore place, any empty barrel can give forth sound, any briar can tear a man's flesh. No flies will go down your throat if you keep your mouth shut, and no evil speaking will come out. Think much, but say little: be quick at work and slow at talk; and above all, ask the great Lord to set a watch over your lips.

7
On Seizing Opportunities

Some men are never awake when the train starts, but crawl into the station just in time to see that everybody is off and then sleepily say, "Dear me, is the train gone? My watch must have stopped in the night." They always come into town a day after the fair, and open their wares an hour after the market is over. They make their hay when the sun has left off shining and cut their corn as soon as the fine weather is ended.; they cry, "Hold hard!" after the shot has left the gun, and lock the stable door when the steed is stolen. They are like a cow's tail, always behind; they take time by the heels, and not by the forelock, if indeed they ever take him at all. They are no more worth than an old almanac; their time has gone for being of use; but unfortunately, you cannot throw them away as you would the almanac, for they are like the cross old lady who had an annuity left her, and meant to take out the full value of it; they won't die, though they are of no use alive. Take-it-easy and Live-long are first cousins, they say, and the more's the pity. If they are immortal till their work is done, they will not die in a hurry, for they have not even begun to work yet. Shiftless people generally excuse their laziness by saying, "they are only a little behind"; but a little too late is much too late, and a miss is as good as a mile. My neighbour Sykes covered up his well after his child was drowned in it; and was very busy down at the Old Farm bringing up buckets of water after every stick of the house had been burnt; one of these days, he'll be for making a will when he can't hold a pen, and he'll be trying to repent of his sins when his senses are going.

These slow coaches think that tomorrow is better than today and take for their rule an old proverb turned topsy-turvy—"Never do today what you can put off till tomorrow." They are forever waiting until their ship comes home and always dreaming about things looking up by-and-by; while grass grows in their furrows and the cows get through the gaps in their hedges. If the birds would but wait to have salt put on their tails, what a breakfast they would take home to their families! but while things move as fast they do, the youngsters at home will have to fill their mouths with empty spoons. "Never mind," say they, "there are better times coming, wait a little longer." Their birds are all in the bush, and rare fat ones they are, according to their account; and so they had need to be, for they have had none in the hand yet, and wife and children are half-starved. Something will turn up, they say: why don't the stupids go and turn it up themselves? Time and tide wait for no man, and yet these fellows loiter about as if they had a freehold of time, a lease of their lives, and a rabbit warren full of opportunities. They will find out their mistake when want finds *them* out, and that will not be long with some in our village, for they are already a long way on the road to Needham. They who would not plough must not expect to eat; they who waste the spring will have a lean autumn. They would not strike when the iron was hot, and they will soon find the cold iron very hard.

"He that will not when he may,
When he will he shall have nay."

Time is not tied to a post, like a horse to a manger; it passes like the wind, and he who would grind his corn by it must set the mill-sails. He that gapes till he be fed, will gape till he be dead. Nothing is to be got without pains except poverty and dirt. In the old days, they said, "Jack gets on by his stupidity." Jack would find it very different nowadays, I think; but never in old times, or any other times, would Jack get on by foolishly letting present chances slip by him; for hares never run into the mouths of sleeping dogs. He that hath time, and looks for better time, time comes that he repents himself of time. There's no good in lying down and crying, "God help us!" God helps those who help themselves. When I see a man who declares that the times are bad, and that he is always unlucky, I generally say to myself, "That old goose did not sit on the eggs till they were all addled, and now providence is to be blamed because they won't hatch." I never had any faith in luck at all, except that I believe good luck will carry a man over a ditch if he jumps well, and will put a bit of bacon into his pot if he looks after his garden and keeps a pig. Luck generally comes to those who look after it, and my notion is that it taps at least once in a lifetime at everybody's door, but if industry does not open it, away it goes. Those who have lost the last coach, and let every opportunity slip by them, turn to abusing providence for setting everything against them: "If I were a hatter," says one, "men would be born without heads." "If I went to the sea for water," quoth another, "I should find it dried up." Every wind is foul for a crazy ship. Neither the wise nor the wealthy can help him who has long refused to help himself.

John Ploughman in the most genteel manner sends his compliments to his friends, and now that harvest is over, and the hops all picked, according to promise, he intends giving them a bit of poetry, just to show that he is trying the polishing brushes. John asked the minister to lend him one of the poets, and he gave him the works of George Herbert, very good, no doubt, but rather tangled, like Harkaway Wood; still, there's a good deal in the queer old verses, and every now and then one comes upon clusters of the sweetest nuts, but some of them are rather hard to crack. The following verse is somewhat near the subject now in hand, and is plain enough in *reason*, though, begging the poet's pardon, John can't see *a rhyme* in it; however, as it is by the great Herbert, it must be good, and will do well enough to ornament John's talk, like a flower stuck in a buttonhole of his Sunday coat.

> "Let thy mind still be bent, still plotting where,
> And when, and how thy business may be done.
> Slackness breeds worms; but the sure traveller,
> Though he alight sometimes, still goeth on.
> Acting and stirring spirits live alone:
> Write on the others, *Here lies such a one*."

8
On Keeping One's Eyes Open

To get through this world, a man must look about him, and even sleep with one eye open; for there are many baits for fishes, many nets for birds, and many traps for men. While foxes are so common, we must not be geese. There is a very great difference in this matter among people of my acquaintance: many see more with one eye than others with two, and many have fine eyes and cannot see a jot. All heads are not sense-boxes. Some are so cunning that they suspect everybody, and so live all their lives in miserable fear of their neighbours; others are so simple that every knave takes them in, and makes his penny of them. One man tries to see through a brick wall and hurts his eyes; while another finds out a hole in it, and sees as far as he pleases. Some work at the mouth of a furnace, and are never scorched; and others burn their hands at the fire when they only mean to warm them. Now, it is true that no one can give another experience, and we must all pick up wit for ourselves; yet I shall venture to give some of the homely cautions which have served my turn, and in the hope that perhaps they may be of use to others as they have been to me.

Nobody is more like an honest man than a thorough rogue. When you see a man with a great deal of religion displayed in his shop window, you may depend upon it he keeps a very small stock of it within. Do not choose your friend by his looks: handsome shoes often pinch the feet. Don't be fond of compliments: remember, "Thank you, pussy, and thank you, pussy," killed the cat. Don't believe in the man who talks most, for mewing cats are very seldom good mousers. By no means put yourself in another person's power: if you put your thumb between two grinders, they are very apt to bite. Drink nothing without seeing it; sign nothing without reading it, and make sure that it means no more than it says. Don't go to law unless you have nothing to lose; lawyers' houses are built on fools' heads. In any business never wade into water where you cannot see the bottom. Put no dependence upon the label of a bag; and count money after your own kin. See the sack opened before you buy what is in it; for he who trades in the dark asks to be cheated. Keep clear of the man who does not value his own character. Beware of everyone who swears: he who would blaspheme his Maker, would make no bones of lying or stealing. Beware of no man more than of yourself, for we often carry our worst enemies within us.

When a new opinion or doctrine comes before you, do not bite till you know whether it is bread or a stone; do not be sure that the gingerbread is good because of the gilt on it. Never shout "hello!" till you are quite out of the wood; and don't cry fried fish till they are caught in the net. There's always time enough to boast—wait a little longer. Don't throw away dirty water till you have got clean; keep on at scraping the roads till you can get better work; for the poorest pay is better than none, and the humblest office is better than being out of employment. Always give up the road to bulls and madmen; and never fight with a coalheaver or contend with a base character for they will be sure to blacken you.

> "Neither trust nor contend,
> Nor lay wagers, nor lend,
> And you may depend
> You'll have peace to your end."

I cannot say quite so much as that old rhyme does, for there's more than that wanted to give peace, but certainly it will help to it. Never ride a broken-kneed horse; the trader who has once been a fraudulent bankrupt, is not the man for you to deal with. A rickety chair is a dangerous seat.

Be shy of people who are over polite, and don't be too fast with those who are forward and rough. When you suspect a design in anything, be on your guard; set the trap as soon as you smell a rat, but mind that you don't catch your own fingers in it. Have very little to do with a boaster, for his beer is all froth, and though he brags that all his goods, and even his copper kettles are gold and silver, you will soon find out that a boaster and a liar are first cousins. Commit all your secrets to no man; trust in God with all your heart, but let your confidence in friends be weighed in the balances of prudence, seeing that men are but men, and all men are frail. Trust not great weights to slender threads. Yet be not evermore suspicious, for suspicion is a cowardly virtue at best. Men are not angels, remember that; but they are not devils, and it is too bad to think them so. One thing be sure of, never believe in any priest of any religion: for before a man could be bad enough to pretend to be a priest, he must have hardened his heart and blinded his conscience to the most horrible degree. Our governors imprison gypsies for telling fortunes, and yet they give fat pensions to those vagabonds who deceive the people in much weightier things. "Bad company" said the thief, as he went to the gallows between the hangman and a priest; a very honest speech, and a very true word, though spoken in jest. It is the ignorance of fools which keeps the pot boiling for priests. May God clean this land from the plague of their presence and make men wise enough to see through their crafty devices. Lastly, my advice to all is—remember that good wisdom is that which will turn out to be wise in the end; seek it, friends, and seek it at the hands of the wisest of all teachers, the Lord Jesus. Trust Him, and He will never fail you; be guided by His word, and it will never mislead you; pray in His name, and your requests will be granted. Remember, he that leans on man will find him a broken reed, but he who builds on Christ has a firm foundation. You may follow Jesus with your eyes shut, if you please; but when others guide you, keep all your eyes open even if you have a dozen and all of them as powerful as telescopes.

9
Thoughts about Thought

Very little of this paper is to be set down to the account of John Ploughman, for our minister, as I may say, found the horses and held the plough handles, and the ploughman only put in a smack of the whip every now and then, just to keep folks awake. "Two heads are better than one," said the woman, when she took her dog with her to market: begging his pardon, our minister is the woman, and the only sensible head in the whole affair. He is a man who is used to giving his people many things of a very different sort from anything which a ploughman is likely to turn out of his wallet; but I have, at his request, dropped in a few homely proverbs into his thoughts, as he says, "by way of salt", which is his very kind way of putting it. I only hope I have not spoiled his writing with my rough expressions. If he thinks well of it, I should like a few more of his pieces to tack my sayings to; and the public shall always be honestly told whether the remarks are to be considered as altogether "John Ploughman's Talk," or as the writings of two characters rolled into one.

There are not so many hours in a year as there may be thoughts in an hour. Thoughts fly in flocks, like starlings, and swarm like bees. Like the withered leaves in autumn, there is no counting them; and like the links in a chain, one draws on another. What a restless being man is! His thoughts dance up and down like midges in a summer's evening. Like a clock full of wheels, with the pendulum in full swing, his mind moves as fast as time flies. This makes thinking such an important business. Many littles make much; and so many light thoughts make a great weight of sin. A grain of sand is light enough, but Solomon tells us that a heap of sand is heavy. Where there are so many children, the mother had need look well after them. We ought to mind our thoughts, for if they turn to be our enemies, they will be too many for us and will drag us down to ruin. Thoughts from heaven, like birds in spring, will fill our souls with music; but thoughts of evil will sting us like vipers.

There is a notion abroad that thought is free; but I remember reading, that although thoughts are toll-free, they are not hell-free; and that saying quite agrees with the good old Book. We cannot be summoned before an earthly court for thinking, but depend upon it we shall have to be tried for it at the Last Judgment. Evil thoughts are the marrow of sin; the malt that sin is brewed from; the tinder which catches the sparks of the devil's temptations! the churn in which the milk of imagination is churned into purpose and plan; the nest in which all evil birds lay their eggs. Be certain, then, that as sure as fire burns brushwood as well as logs, God will punish thoughts of sin as well as deeds of sin.

Let no one suppose that thoughts are not known to the Lord; for He has a window into the closest closet of the soul; a window to which there are no shutters. As we watch bees in a glass hive, so does the eye of the Lord see us. The Bible says, "Hell and destruction are before the Lord: how much more then the hearts of the children of men?" Man is all outside to God. With heaven there are no secrets. That which is done in the private chamber of the heart is as public as the streets before the all-seeing eye.

But some will say that they cannot help having bad thoughts; that may be, but the question is, do they hate them or not? We cannot keep thieves from looking in at our windows, but if we open our doors to them and receive them joyfully, we are as bad as they. We cannot help the birds flying over our heads; but we may keep them from building their nests in our hair. Vain thoughts will knock at the door, but we must not open to them. Though sinful thoughts *rise*, they must not *reign*. He who turns a morsel over and over in his mouth, does so because he likes the flavour, and he who meditates upon evil, loves it, and is ripe to commit it. Think of the devil, and he will appear; turn your thoughts towards sin and your hands will soon follow. Snails leave their slime behind them, and so do vain thoughts. An arrow may fly through the air, and leave no trace; but an ill thought always leaves a trail like a serpent. Where there is much traffic of bad thinking, there will be much mire and dirt: every wave of wicked thought adds something to the corruption which rots upon the shore of life. It is dreadful to think that a vile imagination, once indulged, gets the key of our minds, and can get in again very easily, whether we will or no, and can so return as to bring seven other spirits with it more wicked than itself; and what may follow, no one knows. Nurse sin on the knees of thought, and it will grow into a giant. Dip tow in naphtha, and how it will blaze when fire gets to it! lay a man asoak in depraved thought, and he is ready to flame up into open sin as soon as ever opportunity occurs. This shows us the wisdom of watching, every day, the thoughts and imaginations of our hearts. Good thoughts are blessed guests, and should be heartily welcomed, well fed, and much sought after. Like rose leaves, they give out a sweet smell if laid up in the jar of memory. They cannot be too much cultivated; they are a crop which enriches the soil. As the hen broods her chickens under wings, so should we cherish all holy thoughts. As the poor man's ewe lamb ate of his own bread and lay in his bosom, even so should godly meditation be very dear to us. Holy thoughts breed holy words and holy actions, and are hopeful evidences of a renewed heart. Who would not have them? To keep chaff out of a bushel, one sure plan is to fill it full of wheat; and to keep out vain thoughts, it is wise and prudent to have the mind stored with choice subjects for meditation: these are easy to find, and we should never be without them. May we all be able to say with David, "In the multitude of my thoughts within me, Thy comforts delight my soul."

10
Faults

He who boasts of being perfect is perfect in folly. I have been a good deal up and down in the world, and I never did see either a perfect horse or a perfect man, and I never shall till two Sundays come together. You cannot get white flour out of a coal sack, nor perfection out of human nature; he who looks for it had better look for sugar in the sea. The old saying is, "Lifeless, faultless:" of dead men we should say nothing but good, but as for the living, they are all tarred more or less with the black brush, and half an eye can see it. Every head has a soft place in it, and every heart has its black drop. Every rose has its prickles, and every day its night. Even the sun shows spots, and the skies are darkened with clouds. Nobody is so wise but he has folly enough to stock a stall at Vanity Fair. Where I could not see the fool's cap, I have nevertheless heard the bells jingle. As there is no sunshine without some shadows, so is all human good mixed up with more or less of evil, even poor law guardians have their little failings, and parish beadles are not wholly of heavenly nature.

The best wine has its lees. All men's faults are not written on their foreheads, and it's quite as well they are not, or hats would need very wide brims; yet, as sure as eggs are eggs, faults of some sort nestle in every bosom. There's no telling when a man's sins may show themselves, for hares pop out of the ditch just when you are not looking for them. A horse that is weak in the legs may not stumble for a mile or two, but it is in him, and the rider had better hold him up well. The tabby cat is not lapping milk just now, but leave the dairy door open, and we will see if she is not as bad a thief as the kitten. There's fire in the flint, cool as it looks: wait till the steel gets a knock at it, and you will see. Everybody can read that riddle, but it is not everybody that will remember to keep his gunpowder out of the way of the candle.

If we would always recollect that we live among men who are imperfect, we should not be in such a fever when we find out our friends' failings; what's rotten will rend, and cracked pots will leak. Blessed is he who expects nothing of poor flesh and blood, for he shall never be disappointed. The best of men are men at the best, and the best wax will melt.

> It is a good horse that never stumbles,
> And a good wife that never grumbles.

But surely such horses and wives are only found in the fool's paradise, where dumplings grow on trees. In this wicked world the straightest timber has knots in it, and the cleanest field of wheat has its share of weeds. The most careful driver one day upsets the cart, the cleverest cook spills a little broth, and as I know to my sorrow a very decent ploughman will now and then break the plough and often make a crooked furrow. It is foolish to turn off a tried friend because of a failing or two, for you may get rid of a one-eyed nag and buy a blind one. Being all of us full of faults, we ought to keep two bears, and learn to bear and forbear with one another, since we all live in glass houses, we should none of us throw stones. Everybody laughs when the saucepan says to the kettle, "How black you are!" Other men's imperfections show us our imperfections for one sheep is much like another; and if there's an apple in my neighbour's eye, there is no doubt one in mine. We ought to use our neighbours as looking-glasses to see our own faults in, and mend in ourselves what we see in them.

I have no patience with those who poke their noses into every man's house to smell out his faults, and put on magnifying glasses to discover their neighbours' flaws; such folks had better look at home, they might see the devil where they little expected. What we wish to see, we shall see or think we see. Faults are always thick where love is thin. A white cow is all black if your eye chooses to make it so. If we sniff long enough at rose water, we shall find out that it has a bad smell. It would be a far more pleasant business, at least for other people, if fault hunters would turn their dogs to hunt out the good points in other folks; the game would pay better, and nobody would stand with a pitchfork to keep the huntersmen off his farm. As for our own faults, it would take a large slate to hold the account of them, but, thank God, we know where to take them and how to get the better of them. With all our faults, God loves us still if we are trusting in His Son, therefore, let us not be downhearted, but hope to live and learn and do some good service before we die.

Though the cart creaks it will get home with its load, and the old horse, broken-kneed as he is, will do a sight of work yet. There's no use in lying down and doing nothing because we cannot do everything as we should like. Faults or no faults, ploughing must be done; imperfect people must do it too, or there will be no harvest next year. Bad ploughman as John may be, the angels won't do his work for him, and so he is off to do it himself. Go along, Violet! Gee, whoa! Dapper!

11
Things Not Worth Trying

That is a wise old saying, "Spend not all you have; believe not all you hear; tell not all you know, and do not all you can." There is so much work to be done that needs our hands that it is a pity to waste a grain of our strength. When the game is not worth the candle, drop it at once. It is wasting time to look for milk in a gate-post, or blood in a turnip, or sense in a fool. Never ask a covetous man for money till you have boiled a flint soft. Don't sue a debtor who has not a penny to bless himself with—you will only be throwing good money after bad, which is like losing your ferret without getting a rabbit. Never offer a looking-glass to a blind man: if a man is so proud that he will not see his faults, he will only quarrel with you for pointing them out to him. It is of no use to hold a lantern to a mole, or to talk of heaven to a man who cares for nothing but his dirty money. There's a time for everything, and it is a silly thing to preach to drunken men, it is casting pearls before swine, get them sober and then talk to them soberly; if you lecture them while they are drunk, you act as if you were drunk yourself.

Do not put a cat on a coachbox, or men in places for which they are not fitted. There's no making apples of plums: little minds will still be little, even if you make them beadles or churchwardens. It's a pity to turn a monkey into a minister or a maidservant into a mistress. Many preachers are good tailors spoiled, and capital shoe-makers turned out of their proper calling. When God means a creature to fly, He gives it wings, and when He intends men to preach, he gives them abilities. It is a pity to push a man into the war if he cannot fight. Better discourage a man's climbing than help him to break his neck. Silk purses are not to be made out of sows' ears, and pigs will never play well on the flute, teach them as long as you like.

It is not wise to aim at impossibilities—it is a waste of powder to fire at the man in the moon. Making deal boards out of sawdust is a very sensible scheme compared with what some of my friends have been aiming at, for they have been trying to get money by buying shares in bubble companies; they might quite as soon catch the wind in a net, or carry water in a sieve. Bubbles are fine fun for boys, but bubble companies are edged tools that none should play with. If my friend has money which he can afford to lose, there is still no reason why he should hand it over to a set of knaves: if I wanted to get rid of my leg, I should not get a shark to snap it off for me. Give your money to fools sooner than let rogues wheedle you out of it.

It is never worthwhile to do unnecessary things. Never grease a fat sow or praise a proud man. Don't make clothes for fishes, or coverings for altars. Don't paint lilies or garnish the gospel. Never bind up a man's head before it is broken, or comfort a conscience that makes no confession. Never hold up a candle to show the sun or try to prove a thing which nobody doubts. I would advise no one to attempt a thing which will cost more than it is worth. You may sweeten a dunghill with lavender water, and a bad living man may keep up a good character by an outward show of religion, but it will turn out a losing business in the long run.

If our nation were sensible, it would sweep out a good many expensive but useless people, who eat the malt which lies in the house that Jack built; they live on the national estate, but do it little service. There is very little wisdom in paying a man a pound for earning a penny. If my master's old dog was as sleepy as some folks are, he would get shot or drowned, for he wouldn't be worth the amount of the dog-tax. However, their time of reckoning is on the road, as sure as Christmas is coming.

Long ago my experience taught me not to dispute with anybody about tastes and whims; one might as well argue about what you can see in the fire. It is of no use ploughing the air, or trying to convince a man against his will in matters of no consequence. It is useless to try to end a quarrel by getting angry over it; it is much the same as pouring oil on a fire to quench it, and blowing coals with the bellows to put them out.

Some people like rows—I don't envy their choice; I'd rather walk ten miles to get out of a dispute than half-a-mile to get into one. I have often been told to be bold, and take the bull by the horns, but, as I am inclined to think that the amusement is more pleasant than profitable, I shall leave it to those who are so cracked already that an ugly poke with a horn would not damage their skulls.

Solomon says, "Leave off strife before it be meddled with," which is much the same as if he had said, "Leave off before you begin." When you see a mad dog, don't argue with him unless you are sure of your logic; better get out of his way, and if anybody calls you a coward, you need not call him a fool—everybody knows that. Meddling in quarrels never answers; let hornets' nests alone, and don't pull down old houses over your own head. Meddlers are sure to hurt their own characters: if you scrub other people's pigs, you will soon need scrubbing yourself. It is the height of folly to interfere between a man and his wife, for they will be sure to leave off fighting each other and turn their whole strength upon you—and serve you right, too; if you put your spoon into other people's broth and it scalds you, who is to blame but yourself?

One thing more, don't attempt to make a strong-headed woman give way, but remember the old lines:

> "If she will, she will, you may depend on't
> And if she won't, she won't, and there's an end on't"

The other day I cut out of a newspaper a scrap from America, which shall be my tail-piece: "Dip the Mississippi dry with a teaspoon; twist your heel into the toe of your boot; send up fishing-hooks with balloons and fish for stars; get astride a gossamer and chase a comet; when a rain storm is coming down like the cataract of Niagara, remember where you left your umbrella; choke a flea with a brickbat! In short, prove everything hitherto considered impossible to be possible—but never attempt to coax a woman to say she will when she has made up her mind to say she won't."

12
Debt

When I was a very small boy in pinafores, and went to a woman's school, it so happened that I wanted a stick of slate pencil, and had no money to buy it with. I was afraid of being scolded for losing my pencils so often, because I was a real careless little fellow, and so did not dare to ask at home; what then was John to do? There was a little shop in the place where nuts, and tops, and cakes, and balls were sold by old Mrs. Dearson, and sometimes I had seen boys and girls get trusted by the old lady. I argued with myself that Christmas was coming, and that somebody or other would be sure to give me a penny then, and perhaps even a whole silver sixpence. I would, therefore, go into debt for a stick of slate pencil, and be sure to pay at Christmas. I did not feel easy about it, but still I screwed my courage up and went into the shop. One farthing was the amount, I had never owed anything before and my credit was good, the pencil was handed over by the kind dame, and *I was in debt*. It did not please me much, and I felt as if I had done wrong, but I little knew how soon I should smart for it. How my father came to hear of this little stroke of business I never knew, but some little bird or other whistled it to him, and he was very soon down upon me in right

"Then I was marched off to the shop
like a deserter marched into barracks."

earnest. God bless him for it; he was a sensible man and none of your children spoilers; he did not intend to bring up his children to speculate and play at what big rogues call financing, and therefore, he knocked my getting into debt on the head at once, and no mistake. He gave me a very powerful lecture about getting into debt, and how like it was to stealing, and upon the way in which people were ruined by it; and how a boy who would owe a farthing, might one day owe a hundred pounds, and get into prison, and bring his family into disgrace. It was a lecture, indeed; I think I can hear it now, and can feel my ears tingling at the recollection of it.

Then I was marched off to the shop like a deserter being marched back to barracks, feeling dreadfully ashamed because I thought everybody knew I was in debt. The farthing was paid amid many solemn warnings, and the poor debtor was set free like a bird let out of a cage. How sweet it felt to be out of debt! How did my little heart vow and declare that nothing should ever tempt me into debt again! It was a fine lesson, and I have never forgotten it. If all boys were inoculated with the same doctrine when they were young, it would be as good as a fortune to them and save them wagon loads of trouble in later life. God bless my father, say I, and send a breed of such fathers into old England to save her from being eaten up with villainy, for what with companies and schemes, and paper money, the nation is getting to be as rotten as touchwood.

Ever since that early sickening I have hated debt as Luther hated the Pope, and if I say some fierce things about it, you must not wonder. To keep debt, dirt, and the devil out of my cottage has been my greatest wish ever since I set up housekeeping; and although the last of the three has sometimes got in by the door or the window, for the old serpent will wriggle through, smallest crack, yet, thanks to a good wife, hard work, honesty, and scrubbing brushes, the two others have not crossed the threshold. Debt is so degrading, that if I owed a man a penny I would walk twenty miles in the depth of winter to pay him, sooner than feel that I was under an obligation. I should be as comfortable with peas in my shoes, or a hedgehog in my bed, or a snake up my back, as with bills hanging over my head at the grocer's, and the baker's, and the tailor's. Poverty is hard, but debt is horrible; a man might as well have a smoky house and a scolding wife, which are said to be the two worst evils of life. We may be poor, and yet respectable, which John Ploughman and his wife hope they are and will be; but a man in debt cannot even respect himself, and he is sure to be talked about by the neighbours, and that talk will not be much to his credit. Some persons appear to like to be owing money; but I would as soon be a cat up a chimney with the fire alight, or a fox with the hounds at my heels, or a hedgehog on a pitchfork, or a mouse under an owl's claw. An honest man thinks a purse full of other people's money to be worse than an empty one; he cannot bear to eat other people's cheese, wear other people's shirts, and walk about in other people's shoes, neither will he be easy while his wife is decked out in the milliner's bonnets, and wears the flannels. The jackdaw in the peacock's feathers was soon plucked, and borrowers will surely come to poverty—a poverty of the bitterest sort, because there is shame in it.

Living beyond their incomes is the ruin of many of my neighbours; they can hardly afford to keep a rabbit, and must needs drive a pony and chaise. I am afraid extravagance is the common disease of the times, and many professing Christians have caught it, to their shame and sorrow. Good cotton or stuff gowns are not good enough nowadays; girls must have silks and satins, and then there's a bill at the dressmaker's as long as a winter's night, and quite as dismal. Show, style, and smartness run away with a man's means, keep the family poor, and the father's nose down on the grindstone. Frogs try to look as big as bulls and burst themselves. A pound a week apes five hundred a year, and comes to the county court.Men burn the candle at both ends, and then say they are very unfortunate—why don't they put the saddle on the right horse, and say they are extravagant? Economy is half the battle in life; it is not so hard to earn money as to spend it well. Hundreds would never have known *want* if they had not first known *waste*. If all poor men's wives knew how to cook, how far a little might go! Our minister says the French and the Germans beat us hollow in nice cheap cookery. I wish they would send missionaries over to convert our gossiping women into good managers; this is a French fashion which would be a deal more useful than those fine pictures in Mrs. Frippery's window, with ladies rigged out in a new style every month. Dear me! Some people are much too fine nowadays to eat what their fathers were thankful to see on the table, and so they please their palates with costly feeding, come to the workhouse, and expect everybody to pity them. They turned up their noses at bread and butter, and came to eat raw turnips stolen out of the fields. They who live like fighting cocks at other men's costs, will get their combs cut, or perhaps get roasted for it one of these days. If you have a great store of peas, you may put more in the soup; but everybody should fare according to his earnings. He is both a fool and a knave who has a shilling coming in, and on the strength of it spends a pound which does not belong to him. Cut your coat according to your cloth is sound advice; but cutting other people's cloth by running into debt is as like thieving as fourpence is like a groat. If I meant to be a rogue I would deal in marine stores, or be a petty fogging lawyer, or open a loan office, or go out picking pockets, but I would scorn the dirty art of getting into debt without a prospect of being able to pay.

Debtors can hardly help being liars, for they promise to pay when they know they cannot, and when they have made up a lot of false excuses they promise again, and so they lie as fast as a horse can trot.

> "You have debts, and make debts still,
> If you've not lied, lie you will."

Now, if owing leads to lying, who shall say that it is not a most evil thing? Of course there are exceptions, and I do not want bear down hard upon an honest man who is brought down by sickness or heavy losses, but take the rule as a rule, and you will find debt to be a great dismal swamp, a huge mud-hole, a dirty ditch: happy is the man who gets out of it after once tumbling in, but happiest of all is he who has been by God's goodness kept out of the mire altogether. If you once ask the devil to dinner, it will be hard to get him out of the house again; better to have nothing to do with him. Where a hen has laid one egg she is very likely to lay another; when a man is once in debt, he is likely to get into it again; better keep clear of it from the first. He who gets in for a penny will soon be in for a pound, and when a man is over shoes, he is very liable to be over boots. Never owe a farthing, and you will never owe a guinea.

If you want to sleep soundly, buy a bed of a man who is in debt; surely it must be a very soft one, or he never could have rested so easy on it. I suppose people get hardened to it, as Smith's donkey did when its master broke so many sticks across its back. It seems to me that a real honest man would sooner get as lean as a greyhound than feast on borrowed money, and would choke up his throat with March dust before he would let the landlord make chalks against him behind the door for a beer score. What pins and needles tradesmen's bills must stick in a fellow's soul! A pig on credit always grunts. Without debt, without care; out of debt, out of danger; but owing and borrowing are bramble bushes full of thorns. If ever I borrow a spade from my next door neighbour, I never feel safe with it for fear I should break it; I never can dig in peace as I do with my own; but if I had a spade at the shop and knew I could not pay for it, I think I should set to and dig my own grave out of shame. Scripture says, "Owe no man anything," which does not mean pay your debts, but never have any to pay, and my opinion is, that those who wilfully break this law ought to be turned out of the Christian church, neck and crop, as we say. Our laws are shamefully full of encouragement to credit: nobody need be a thief now; he has only to open a shop and make a fail of it, and it will pay him much better; as the proverb is, "He who never fails will never grow rich." Why, I know tradesmen who have failed five or six times, and yet think they are on the road to heaven; the scoundrels, what would they do if they got there? They are a deal more likely to go where they shall never come out till they have paid the uttermost farthing. But people say, "How liberal they are!" Yes, with other people's money. I hate to see a man steal a goose and then give religion the giblets. Piety by all means, but pay your way as part of it. Honesty first, and then generosity. But how often religion is a cloak for deceiving! There's Mrs. Scamp as fine as a peacock, all the girls out at boarding-school learning French and the piano, the boys swelling about in kid gloves, and G. B. Scamp, Esquire, driving a fast-trotting mare, and taking the chair at public meetings, while his poor creditors cannot get more than enough to live from hand to mouth. It is shameful and beyond endurance to see how genteel swindling is winked at by many in this country. I'd off with their white waistcoats, and kid gloves, and patent leather boots, if I had my way, and give them the county crop, and the prison livery for six months; gentlemen or not, I'd let them see that big rogues could dance on the treadmill to the same tune as little ones. I'd make the land too hot to hold such scamping gentry if I were a member of Parliament or a prime minister; as I've no such power, I can at least write against the fellows, and let off the steam of my wrath in that way.

My motto is, pay as you go, and keep from small scores. Short reckonings are soon cleared. Pay what you owe, and what you're worth you'll know. Let the clock tick, but no "*tick*" for me. Better go to bed without your supper than get up in debt. Sins and debts are always more than we think them to be. Little by little a man gets in over head and ears. It is the petty expenses that empty the purse. Money is round, and rolls away easily. Tom Thriftless buys what he does not want because it is a great bargain, and so he is soon brought to sell what he does want, and find it a very little bargain; he cannot say "No" to his friend who wants him to be security; he gives grand dinners, makes many holidays, keeps a fat table, lets his wife dress fine, never looks after his servants, and by-and-by he is quite surprised to find that quarter-days come round so very fast, and that creditors bark so loud. He has sowed his money in the fields of thoughtlessness, and now he wonders that he has to reap the harvest of poverty. Still he hopes for something to turn up to help him out of difficulty, and so muddles himself into more troubles, forgetting that hope and expectation are a fool's income. Being hard up, he goes to market with empty pockets, and buys at whatever prices tradesmen like to charge him, and so he pays more than double and gets deeper and deeper into the mire. This leads him to scheming, and trying little tricks and mean dodges, for it is hard for an empty sack to stand upright. This is sure not to answer, for schemes are like spiders' webs which never catch anything better than flies, and are soon swept away. As well attempt to mend your shoes with brown paper or stop a broken window with a sheet of ice, as try to patch up a falling business with manoeuvering and scheming. When the schemer is found out, he is like a dog in church whom everybody kicks at, and like a barrel of powder which nobody wants for a neighbour.

They say poverty is a sixth sense, and it had need be, for many debtors seem to have lost the other five, or were born without common sense, for they appear to fancy that you not only make debts, but pay them by borrowing. A man pays Peter with what he has borrowed of Paul, and thinks he is getting out of his difficulties, when he is only putting one foot into the mud to pull his other foot out. It is hard to shave an egg or pull hairs out of a bald pate, but they are both easier than paying debts out of an empty pocket. Samson was a strong man, but he could not pay debts without money; and he is a fool who thinks he can do it by scheming. As to borrowing money of loan societies, it's like a drowning man catching at razors: both Jews and Gentiles, when they lend money, generally pluck the geese as long as they have any feathers. A man must cut down his outgoings and save his incomings if he wants to clear himself; you can't spend your penny and pay debts with it too. Stint the kitchen if the purse is bare. Don't believe in any way of wiping out debts except by paying hard cash. Promises make debts, and debts make promises, but promises never pay debts; promising is one thing, and performing is quite another. A good man's word should be as binding as an oath, and he should never promise to pay unless he has a clear prospect of doing so in due time; those who stave off payment by false promises, deserve no mercy. It is all very well to say "I'm very sorry," but—

> "A hundred years of regret
> Pay not a farthing of debt."

Now I'm afraid all this sound advice might as well have been given to my master's cocks and hens as to those who have got into the way of spending what is not their own, for advice to such people goes in at one ear and out at the other; well, those who won't listen will have to feel, and those who refuse cheap advice will have to buy dear repentance; but to young people beginning life, a word may be worth a world, and this shall be John Ploughman's short sermon, with three heads to it— always live a little below your means, never get into debt, and remember—

> He who goes a-borrowing
> Goes a-sorrowing.

13
Home

That word *home* always sounds like poetry to me. It rings like a peal of bells at a wedding, only more soft and sweet, and it chimes deeper into the ears of my heart. It does not matter whether it means thatched cottage or manor house, home is home, be it ever so homely, and there's no place on earth like it. Green grow the houseleek on the roof for ever, and let the moss flourish on the thatch. Sweetly the sparrows chirrup and the swallows twitter around the chosen spot which is my joy and rest. Every bird loves its own nest; the owl thinks the old ruin the fairest spot under the moon, and the fox is of opinion that his hole in the hill is remarkably cosy. When my master's nag knows that his head is towards home, he wants no whip, but thinks it best to put on all steam; and I am always of the same mind, for the way home, to me, is the best bit of road in the country. I like to see the smoke out of my own chimney better than the fire on another man's hearth; there's something so beautiful in the way in which it curls up among the trees. Cold potatoes on my own table taste better than roast meat at my neighbour's, and the honeysuckle at my own door is the sweetest I ever smell. When you are out, friends do their best, but still it is not home. "Make yourself at home," they say, because everybody knows that to feel at home is to feel at ease,

> "East and west
> Home is best."

Why, at home you are at home, and what more do you want? Nobody begrudges you, whatever your appetite may be; and you don't get put into a damp bed. Safe in his own castle, like a king in his palace, a man feels himself somebody, and is not afraid of being thought proud for thinking so. Every cock may crow on his own dunghill; and a dog is a lion when he is at home. A sweep is master inside his own door. No need to guard every word because some enemy is on the watch, no keeping the heart under lock and key; but as soon as the door is shut, it is liberty hall, with none to peep and pry. There is a glorious view from the top of Leith Hill, in our dear old Surrey, and Hindhead, and Martha's Chapel, and Boxhill, are not to be sneezed at; but I could show you something which, to my mind, beats them all to nothing for real beauty. I mean John Ploughman's cottage, with the kettle boiling on the hob, singing like an unfallen black angel, while the cat is lying asleep in front of the fire, and the wife in her chair mending stockings, and the children cutting about the room as full of fun as young lambs. It is a singular fact, perhaps some of you will doubt it, but that is your unbelieving nature, our little ones are real beauties, always a pound or two plumper than others of their age, and yet it doesn't tire you half so much to nurse them as it does other people's babies. Why, bless you, my wife would tire out in half the time if her neighbour had asked her to see to a strange youngster, but her own children don't seem to tire her at all; now my belief is that it all comes of their having been born at home. Just so with everything else: our lane is the most beautiful for twenty miles around,because our home is in it; and my garden is a perfect paradise, for no other reason than this very good one, that it belongs to the old house at home.

I cannot make out why so many working men spend their evenings at the public house, when their own fireside would be so much better and cheaper too. There they sit, hour after hour, boozing and talking nonsense, and forgetting the dear good souls at home who are half starved and weary with waiting for them. Their money goes into the publican's till when it ought to make their wives and children comfortable; as for the beer they get, it is just so much fools' milk to drown their wits in. Such fellows ought to be horsewhipped, and those who encourage them and live on their spendings deserve to feel the butt end of the whip. Those beershops are the curse of this country—no good ever can come of them, and the evil they do no tongue can tell; the publics are bad enough, but the beershops are a pest; I wish the man who made the law to open them had to keep all the families that they have brought to ruin. Beershops are the enemies of home, and therefore the sooner their licences are taken away the better; poor men don't need such places, nor rich men either—they are all worse and no the better, like Tom Norton's wife. Anything that hurts the home is a curse and ought to be hunted down as gamekeepers do the vermin in the copses.

Husbands should try to make home happy and holy. It is an ill bird that fouls its own nest, a bad man who makes his home wretched. Our house ought to be a little church, with holiness to the Lord over the door, but it ought never to be a prison where there is plenty of rule and order, but little love and no pleasure. Married life is not all sugar, but grace in the heart will keep away most of the sours. Godliness and love can make a man, like a bird in a hedge, sing among thorns and briars, and set others singing too. It should be the husband's pleasure to please his wife, and the wife's care to care for her husband. He is kind to himself who is kind to his wife. I am afraid some men live by the rule of self, and when that is the case, home happiness is a mere sham. When husbands and wives are well yoked, how light their load becomes! It is not every couple that is such a pair, and more's the pity. In a true home all the strife is who can do the most to make the family happy. A home should be a Bethel, not a Babel. The husband should be the "houseband," binding together like a cornerstone, but not crushing everything like a millstone. Unkind and domineering husbands ought not to pretend to be Christians, for they act totally contrary to Christ's commands. Yet a home must be well ordered, or it will become a Bedlam and a scandal to the parish. If the father drops the reins, the family coach will soon be in the ditch. A wise mixture of love and firmness will do it, but neither harshness nor softness alone will keep home in happy order.

Home is no home where the children are not in obedience, it is rather a pain than a pleasure to be in it. Happy is he who is happy in his children, and happy are the children who are happy in their father. All fathers are not wise. Some are like Eli, and spoil their children. Not to cross our children is the way to make a cross of them. Those who never give their children the rod, must not wonder if their children become a rod to them. Solomon says, "Correct thy son, and he shall give thee rest; yea, he shall give delight to thy soul." I am not clear that anybody wiser than Solomon lives in our time, though some think they are. Young colts must be broken in or they will make wild horses. Some fathers are all fire and fury, filled with passion at the smallest fault; this is worse than the other, and makes home a little hell instead of a heaven. No wind makes the miller idle, but too much upsets the mill altogether. Men who strike in their anger generally miss their mark. When God helps us to hold the reins firmly, but not to hurt the horses' mouths, all goes well. When home is ruled by God's word, angels might be asked to stay a night with us, and they would not find themselves out of their element.

Wives should feel that home is their place and their kingdom, the happiness of which depends mostly upon them. She is a wicked wife who drives her husband away by her long tongue. A man said to his wife the other day, "Double up your whip;" he meant keep your tongue quiet: it is wretched living with such a whip always lashing you. When God gave to men ten measures of speech, they say the women ran away with nine, and in some cases I am afraid the saying is true. A dirty, slatternly, gossiping wife is enough to drive her husband mad; and if he goes to the public house of an evening, she is the cause of it. It is doleful living where the wife, instead of reverencing her husband, is always wrangling and railing at him. It must be a good thing when such women are hoarse, and it is a pity that they have not as many blisters on their tongues as they have teeth in their jaws. God save us all from wives who are angels in the streets, saints in the church, and devils at home. I have never tasted of such bitter herbs, but I pity from my very heart those who have this diet every day of their lives.

Show me a loving husband, a worthy wife, and good children, and no pair of horses that ever flew along the road could take me in a year where I could see a more pleasing sight. Home is the grandest of all institutions. Talk about parliament, but give me a quiet little parlour. Boast about voting and the reform bill if you like, but I go in for weeding the little garden and teaching, the children their hymns. Franchise may be a very fine thing, but I should a good deal sooner get the freehold of my cottage, if I could find the money to buy it. Magna Charta I don't know much about, but if it means a quiet home for everybody, three cheers for it.

I wish our governors would not break up so many poor men's homes by that abominably heartless poor law. It is far more fit for mad dogs than Englishmen. A Hampshire carter told me the other day that his wife and children were all in the union and his home broken up, because of the cruel working of the poor law. He had eight little ones and his wife to keep on nine shillings a week, with rent to pay out of it; on this he could not keep body and soul together; now, if the parish had allowed him a mere trifle, a loaf or two and a couple of shillings a week, he would have jogged on, but no, not a penny out of the house. They might all die of starvation unless they would all go into the workhouse. So, with many bitter tears and heartaches, the poor soul had to sell his few little bits of furniture, and he is now a houseless man, and yet he is a good hard-working fellow, and served one master for nearly twenty years. Such things are very common, but they ought not to be. Why cannot the really deserving poor have a little help given them? Why must they be forced into the union house? Home is the pillar of the British Empire, and ought not to be knocked to pieces by these unchristian laws. I wish I was an orator and could talk politics, I would not care a rush for the Whigs or Tories, but I would stand up like a lion for the poor man's home, which, let me tell the lords and commons, is as dear to him as their great palaces are to them, and sometimes dearer.

If I had no home the world would be a big prison to me. England for me for a country, Surrey for a county, and for a village give me—no, I shan't tell you, or you will be hunting John Ploughman up. Many of my friends have emigrated, and are breaking up fresh soil in Australia and America. Though their stone has rolled, I hope they may gather moss, for when they were at home they were like the sitting hen, which gets no barley. Really these hard times make a man think of his wings, but I am tied by the leg to my own home, and, please God, I hope to live and die among my own people. They may do things better in France and Germany, but old England for me, after all.

14
Men Who Are Down

No man's lot is fully known till he is dead, change of fortune is the lot of life. He who rides in the carriage may yet have to clean it. Sawyers change places, and he who is up aloft may have to take his turn in the pit. In less than a thousand years we shall all be bald and poor too, and who knows what he may come to before that? The thought that we may ourselves be one day under the window should make us careful when we are throwing out our dirty water. With what measure we mete it shall be measured to us again, and therefore let us look well to our dealings with the unfortunate.

Nothing makes me more sick of human nature than to see the way in which men treat others when they fall down the ladder of fortune. "Down with him," they cry, "He always was good for nothing."

"Down among the dead men, down, down, down,
Down among the dead men, there let him lie."

Dog won't eat dog, but men will eat each other up like cannibals and boast of it too. There are thousands in this world who fly like vultures to feed on a tradesman or a merchant as soon as ever he gets into trouble. Where the carcass is, thither will the eagles be gathered together.

Instead of a little help, they give the sinking man a great deal of cruelty, and cry, "Serves him right." All the world will beat the man whom fortune buffets. If providence smites him, all men's whips begin to crack. The dog is drowning, and therefore all his friends empty their buckets over him. The tree has fallen, and everybody runs for his hatchet. The house is on fire, and all the neighbours warm themselves. The man has ill luck, therefore his friends give him ill usage; he has tumbled into the road, and they drive their carts over him: he is down and selfishness cries, "Let him be kept down, then there will be the more room for those who are up."

How aggravating it is when those who knocked you down, kick you for not standing up! It is not very pleasant to hear that you have been a great fool, and that there were fifty ways at least of keeping out of your difficulty, only you had not the sense to see them. You ought not to have lost the game; even Tom Fool can see where you made a bad move. "*He ought to have locked the stable door;*" everybody can see that, but nobody offers to buy the loser a new nag. "*What a pity he went so far on the ice!*" That's very true, but that won't save the poor fellow from drowning. When a man's coat is threadbare, it is an easy thing to pick a hole in it. Good advice is poor food for a hungry family.

> "A man of words and not of deeds
> Is like a garden full of weeds."

Lend me a bit of string to tie up the traces, and find fault with my old harness when I get home. Help my old horse to a few oats, and then tell him to mend his pace. Feel for me, and I shall be much obliged to you, but mind you feel in your pocket or else a fig for your feelings.

Most men who go downhill meet with Judas before they get to the bottom. Those whom they helped in their better days generally forget the debt, or repay it with unkindness. The young sucker runs away with sap from the old tree. The foal drains his mother, and then kicks her. The old saying is, "I taught you to swim, and now you would drown me," and many a time it comes true. The dog wags his tail till he gets the bone, and then he snaps and bites at the man who fed him. Eaten bread is forgotten, and the hand that gave it is despised. The candle lights others and is burnt away itself. For the most part, nothing is more easily blotted out than a good turn. Everyone for himself is the world's golden rule, and we all know who takes the hindmost. The fox looks after his own skin, and has no idea of losing his brush out of gratitude to a friend.

A noble spirit always takes the side of the weak, but noble spirits do not often ride along our roads; they are as scarce as eagles; you can get magpies, and hawks, and kites by the score, but the nobler breed you don't see once in a lifetime. Did you ever hear the crows read the burial service over a dead sheep before they eat it? Well, that's wonderfully like the neighbours crying, "What a pity! How did it happen? Oh, dear! Oh, dear!" and then falling to work to get each of them a share of the plunder. Most people will help those who do not need it; every traveller throws a stone where there is a heap already; all the cooks baste the fat pig, and the lean one gets burned.

"In times of prosperity friends will be plenty:
In times of adversity not one in twenty."

When the wind serves, all aid. While the pot boils, friendship blooms. But flatterers haunt not cottages, and the faded rose no suitor knows. All the neighbours are cousins to the rich man, but the poor man's brother does not know him. When we have a ewe and a lamb, everyone cries, "Welcome, Peter!" The squire can be heard for half-a-mile, if he only whispers, but Widow Needy is not heard across the park railings, let her call as she may. Men willingly pour water into a full tub and give feasts to those who are not hungry, because they look to have as good or better in return. Have a goose and get a goose. Have a horse of your own, and then you can borrow one. It is safe to lend barley when the barn is full of wheat, but who lends or gives where there's none? Who, indeed, unless it be some antiquated old soul who believes in his Bible and loves his Lord, and therefore gives, "hoping for nothing again?"

I have noticed certain gentry who pretend to be great friends to a falling man because there are some few pickings yet to be got off his bones. The lawyer and the money-lender will cover the poor fellow with their wings and then peck at him with their bills till there's nothing left. When these folks are very polite and considerate, poor men had need beware. It was not a good sign when the fox walked into the hen-roost and said, "Good morning to you all, my very dear friends."

Down men, however, must not despair, for God is yet alive, and He is the friend of the friendless. If there be no one else found to hold out a hand to him who has fallen, the Lord's hand shall not fail to bring deliverance to those who trust Him. A good man may be put in the fire but he cannot be burned. His hope may be drenched but not drowned. He plucks up courage and sets a stout heart to a stiff hill, and gets over rough ground where others lie down and die. While there's life there's hope. Therefore, my friend, if you've tumbled off the back of prosperity, John Ploughman bids you not to lie in the ditch, but up with you and try again. Jonah went to the bottom of the sea but he got to shore again all the better for his watery journey.

> "Though the bird's in the net,
> It may get away yet;
> Though I'm down in the dust,
> In my God I will trust,
> I will hope in Him still,
> And leave all to His will;
> For He'll surely appear,
> And will banish my fear."

Let it never be forgotten that when a man is down, he has a grand opportunity for trusting in God. A false faith can only float in smooth water; but true faith, like a lifeboat, is at home in storms. If our religion does not bare us up in time of trial, what is the use of it? If we cannot believe God when our circumstances appear to be against us, we do not believe Him at all. We trust a thief as far as we can see him; shall we dare to treat our God in that fashion? No, no. The Lord is good, and He will yet appear for His servants, and we shall praise His name.

"Down among the dead men"!
No, sir, not I.
"Down among the dead men"!
I will not lie.
Up among the hopeful,
I will ascend,
Up among the joyful,
sing without end.

15
Hope

Eggs are eggs, but some are rotten; and so hopes are hopes, but many of them are delusions. Hopes are like women, there is a touch of angel about them, but there are two sorts. My boy Tom has been blowing a lot of birds' eggs, and threading them on a string; I have been doing the same thing with hopes, and here's a few of them, good, bad and indifferent.

The sanguine man's hope pops up in a moment like jack-in-the-box; it works with a spring, and does not go by reason. Whenever this man looks out of the window, he sees better times coming and although it is nearly all in his own eye and nowhere else, yet to see plum puddings in the moon is a far more cheerful habit than croaking at everything like a two-legged frog. This is the kind of brother to be on the road with on a pitch-dark night when it pours with rain, for he carries candles in his eyes, and a fireside in his heart. Beware of being misled by him, and then you may safely keep his company. His fault is that he counts his chickens before they are hatched and sells his herrings before they are in the net. All his sparrow's eggs are bound to turn into thrushes, at the least, if not partridges and pheasants. Summer has fully come, for he has seen one swallow. He is sure to make his fortune at his new shop, for he had not opened the door five minutes before two of the neighbours crowded in, one of them wanted a loaf of bread on trust, and the other asked change for a shilling. He is certain that the squire means to give him his custom, for he saw him reading the name over the shop door as he rode past. He does not believe in slips between cups and lips, but makes certainties out of perhapses. Well, good soul, though he is a little soft at times, there is much in him to praise, and I like to think of one of his old sayings, "Never say *die* till you are dead, and then it's no use, so let it alone." There are other odd people in the world, you see, besides John Ploughman.

My neighbour, Shiftless, is waiting for his aunt to die, but the old lady has as many lives as nine cats, and my notion is that when she does die she will leave her little money to the Hospital for Diseased Cats or Stray Dogs, sooner than her nephew Jack shall have it. Poor creature, he is dreadfully down at the heel, and lays it all on the dear old lady's provoking constitution. However, he hopes on and gets worse and worse, for while the grass grows the horse starves. He pulls at a long rope who waits for another's death; he who hunts after legacies had need have iron shoes. He that waits for dead men's shoes may long go barefoot; he who waits for his uncle's cow need not be in a hurry to spread the butter. He who lives on hope has a slim diet.

If Jack Shiftless had never had an aunt, he might have tucked up his shirt sleeves and worked for himself, but they told him he was born with a silver spoon in his mouth, and that made a spoon of him, so that he is no more use at work than a cow catching hares.

If anybody likes to leave John Ploughman a legacy, he will be very much obliged to them, but they had better not tell him of it for fear he should not plough so straight a furrow; they had better make it twice as much and take him by surprise. On the whole, it would be better to leave it to the Pastor's College or the Stockwell Orphanage, for it will be well used in either case. I wish people would think less about windfalls and plant more apple trees. Hopes that grow out of graves are grave mistakes; and when they cripple a man's own energies, they are a sort of hangman's rope, dangling round a man's neck.

Some people are born on the first of April, and are always hoping without sense or reason. Their ship is to come home; they are to dig up a pot of gold, or to hear something to their advantage. Poor sillies, they have wind on the brain, and dream while they are awake. They may hold their mouths open a long while before fried ham and eggs will come flying into them, and yet they really seem to believe that some stroke of luck, some windfall of golden apples, will one day set them up and make gentlemen of them. They hope to ride in their coaches, and by-and-by find themselves shut up in a place where the coaches won't run over them. You may whistle a long while before goldfinches will hop on to your thumb. Once in a while one man in a million may stumble against a fortune, but thousands ruin themselves by idle expectations. Expect to get half of what you earn, a quarter of what is your due, and none of what you have lent, and you will be near the mark; but to look for a fortune to fall from the moon is to play the fool with a vengeance. A man ought to hope within the bounds of reason and the promises

"They may hold their mouths open a long while
before fried ham and eggs will come flying into them."

of the good old Book. Hope leans on an anchor, but an anchor must have something to hold by and to hold to. A hope without grounds is a tub without a bottom, a horse without a head, a goose without a body, a shoe without a sole, a knife without a blade. Who but Simple Simon would begin to build a house at the top? There must be a foundation. Hope is no hope, but sheer folly,when a man hopes for impossibilities, or looks for crops without sowing seed, and for happiness without doing good. Such hopes lead to great boast and small roast; they act like a jack-o'-lantern and lead men into the ditch. There's poor Will at the workhouse who always declares that he owns a great estate, only the right owner keeps him out of it; his name is Jenyns, or Jennings, and somebody of that name he says has left enough money to buy the Bank of England, and one day he is to have a share of it. But meanwhile poor Will finds the parish broth poor stuff for such a great gentleman's stomach; he has promised me an odd thousand or two when he gets his fortune, and I am going to build a castle in the air with it, and ride to it on a broomstick. Poor soul, like a good many others he has windmills in his head, and may make his will on his thumbnail for anything that he has to give. Depend upon it, ploughing the air is not half so profitable as it is easy: he who hopes in this world for more than he can get by his own earnings hopes to find apricots on a crab-tree. He who marries a slovenly, dressy girl, and hopes to make her a good wife might as well buy a goose and expect it to turn out a milch cow. He who takes his boys to the beershop and trusts that they will grow up sober puts his coffee-pot on the fire and expects to see it look bright as new tin. Men cannot be in their senses when they brew with bad malt and look for good beer, or set a wicked example and reckon upon raising a respectable family. You may hope and hope till your heart grows sick; but when you send your boy up the chimney, he'll come down black for all your hoping. Teach a child to lie, and then hope that he will grow up honest; better put a wasp in a tar barrel and wait till he makes you honey. When will people act sensibly with their boys and girls? Not till they are sensible themselves.

As to the next world, it is a great pity that men do not take a little more care when they talk of it. If a man dies drunk, somebody or other is sure to say, "I hope he is gone to heaven." It is all very well to wish it, but to hope it, is another thing. Men turn their faces to hell, and hope to get to heaven; why don't they walk into the horse pond and hope to be dry? Hopes of heaven are solemn things and should be tried by the word of God. A man might as well hope, as our Lord says, to gather grapes of thorns or figs of thistles as look for a happy hereafter at the end of a bad life. There is only one rock to build good hopes on, and that is not Peter, as the Pope says, neither is it the sacraments, but the merits of the Lord Jesus. All the hope of man is in "the man Christ Jesus." If we believe in him we are saved, for it is written, "he that believeth in him hath everlasting life." Mind he has it now, and it is everlasting, so that there is no fear of his losing it. There John Ploughman rests, and he is not afraid, for this is a firm footing, and gives him hope sure and steadfast, which neither life nor death can shake; but John must not turn preacher, so please remember that presumption is a ladder which will break the mounter's neck, and don't try it, as you love your soul.

16
Spending

To earn money is easy compared with spending it well; anybody may dig up potatoes, but it is not one woman in ten that can cook them. Men do not become rich by what they get but by what they save. Many men who have money are as short of wit as a hog is of wool; they are under the years of discretion though they have turned forty, and make ducks and drakes of hundreds as boys do of stones. What their fathers got with the rake they throw away with the shovel. After the miser comes the prodigal. Often men say of the spendthrift, that his old father was no man's friend but his own, and now the son is no man's enemy but his own: the fact is, the old gentleman went to hell by the lean road, and his son has made up his mind to go there by the fat. As soon as the spendthrift gets his estate it goes like a lump of butter in a greyhound's mouth. All his days are the first of April; he would buy an elephant at a bargain, or thatch his house with pancakes, nothing is too foolish to tickle his fancy; his money burns holes in his pocket, and he must squander it, always boasting that his motto is, "Spend, and God will send." He will not stay till he has his sheep before he shears them; he forestalls his income, draws upon his capital, and so kills the goose which lays the golden eggs, and cries out, "who would have thought it?" He never spares at the brim, but he means, he says, to save at the bottom. He borrows at high interest of Rob'em, Cheat'em, and Sell'em-up, and when he gets cleaned out, he lays it all either upon the lawyers or else on the bad times. Times never were good for lazy prodigals, and if they were good to them, they would be bad for all the world besides. Why men should be in such a hurry to make themselves beggars is a mystery, but nowadays, what with betting at horse races, laziness, and speculating, there seems to be a regular four-horse coach running to Needham every day. Ready-money must be quite a curiosity to some men, and yet they spend like lords. They are gentlemen without means, which is much the same as plum-puddings without plums.

> Spending your money with many a guest,
> Empties the larder, the cellar, and chest.

If a little gambling is thrown in with the fast living, money melts like a snowball in an oven. A young gambler is sure to be an old beggar if he lives long enough.

> The devil leads him by the nose,
> Who the dice so often throws.

There are more asses than those with four legs. I am sorry to say they are found among working men as well as fine gentlemen. Fellows who have no estate but their labour, and no family arms except those they work with, will yet spend their little hard earnings at the bar or in waste. No sooner are their wages paid than away they go to the "Spotted Dog," or the "Marquis of Granby," to contribute their share of fools' pence towards keeping up the landlord's red face and round potbelly. Drinking water neither makes a man sick nor in debt, nor his wife a widow, and yet some men hardly know the flavour of it; but beer, guzzled down as it is by many a working man is nothing better than brown ruin. Dull droning blockheads sit on the ale bench and wash out what little sense they ever had. However, I believe that farming people are a great deal better managers with their money than Londoners are, for though their money is very little, their families look nice and tidy on Sundays. True, the rent isn't so bad in a village as in the town, and there's a bit of garden; still, those Londoners earn a deal of money, and they have many chances of buying in a cheap market which the poor countryman has not; on the whole, I think very good management which keeps a family going on ten shillings a week in the country, and bad management that can't pay its way on five-and-twenty in London. Why, some families are as merry as mice in malt on very small wages, and others are as wretched as rats in a trap on double the amount. Those who wear the shoe know best where it pinches, but economy is a fine thing, and makes ninepence go further than a shilling. Some make soup out of a flint, and others can't get nourishment out of gravy beef. Some go to shop with as much wit as Samson had in both his shoulders, but no more; they do not buy well; they have not sense to lay out their money to advantage. Buyers ought to have a hundred eyes, but these have not even half a one, and they do not open that; well was it said that if fools did not go to market bad wares would never be sold. They never get a pennyworth for their penny, and this often because they are on the hunt for cheap things, and forget that generally the cheapest is the dearest, and one cannot buy a good shilling's worth of a bad article. When there's five eggs a penny, four of them are rotten. Poor men often buy in very small quantities, and so pay through the nose; for the man who buys by the pennyworth keeps his own house and another man's. Why not get two or three weeks' supply at once, and so get it cheaper? Store is no sore. People are often saving at the wrong place, and spoil the ship for a half penny's worth of tar. Others look after small savings and forget greater things; they are penny wise and pound foolish; they spare at the spigot, and let all run away at the bunghole. Some buy things they don't want because they are great bargains; let me tell them that what they do not want is dear at a farthing. Fine dressing makes a great hole in poor people's means. Whatever does John Ploughman and others as work hard for their daily bread want, with silks and satins? It's like a blacksmith wearing a white silk apron. I hate to see a servant girl or a labourer's daughter decked out as if she thought people would take her for a lady. Why, everybody knows a tadpole from a fish, nobody mistakes a poppy for a rose. Give me a woman in a nice neat dress, clean and suitable, and for beauty she will beat the flashy young hussies all to pieces. If a girl has got a few shillings to spare, let her buy a good bit of flannel for the winter, before she is tempted with bright looking but useless finery. Buy what suits yourself to wear, and if it does not suit other people to look at, let them shut their eyes. All women are good—either for something or for nothing, and their dress will generally tell you which.

I suppose we all find money goes quite fast enough, but after all it was made to circulate, and there's no use in hoarding it. It is bad to see our money becoming a runaway servant and leave us, but it would be worse to have it stop with us and become our master. We should try, as our minister says, "to find the golden mean," and neither be lavish nor stingy. He has his money best spent who has the best wife. The husband may earn money, but only the wife can save it. "A wise woman buildeth her house, but the foolish plucketh it down with her hands." The wife, it seems, according to Solomon, is the builder or the real puller down. A man cannot prosper till he gets his wife's leave. A thrifty housewife is better than a great income. A good wife and health are a man's best wealth. Bless their hearts, what should we do without them? It is said they like to have their own way, but then the proverb says, a wife ought to have her will during life, because she cannot make one when she dies. The weather is so melting that I cannot keep up this talk any longer, and therefore I shall close with an old-fashioned rhyme—

> "Heaven bless the wives, they fill our hives
> With little bees and honey!
> They soothe life's shocks, they mend our socks,
> But don't they spend the money!"

17
A Good Word for Wives

We pulled up the horses in the last chapter at the sign of the "Good Woman," and, as there is good entertainment for man, if not for beast under that sign, we will make a stay of it, and dip our pen into some of that superfine ink which has no galls in it. When he writes on so fair a subject, John Ploughman must be on his best behaviour.

It is astonishing how many old sayings there are against wives, you may find nineteen to the dozen of them. The men years ago showed the rough side of their tongues whenever they spoke of their spouses. Some of these sayings are downright shocking; as, for instance, that very wicked one, "Every man has two good days with his wife —the day he marries her, and the day he buries her; and that other, "He that loseth his wife and a farthing, has a great loss of the farthing."

I recollect an old ballad that Gaffer Brooks used to sing about a man's being better hung than married, it shows how common it was to abuse the married life. It is almost too bad to print it, but here it is, as near as I can remember it:—

"There was a victim in a cart,
One day for to be hang'd,
And his reprieve was granted,
And the cart made for to stand.

"'Come marry a wife, and save your life,'
The judge aloud did cry;
'Oh, why should I corrupt my life?'
The victim did reply.

"'For here's a crowd of every sort,
And why should I prevent their sport?
The bargain's bad in every part,
The wife's the worst—drive on the cart.'"

Now this rubbish does not prove that the women are bad,
but that their husbands are good for nothing, or else they
would not make up such abominable slanders about their
partners. The rottenest bough cracks first, and it looks as
if the male side of the house was the worse of the two, for
it certainly has made up the most grumbling proverbs.
There have, no doubt, been some shockingly bad wives
in the world, who have been provoking enough to make
a man say,

"If a woman were as little as she is good,
a peashell would make her a gown and a hood."

But how many thousands have there been of true
helpmeets, worth far more than their weight in gold!
There is only one Job's wife mentioned in the Bible and
one Jezebel, but there are no end of Sarahs and Rebekahs.
I am of Solomon's mind that, as a rule, He that findeth
a wife findeth a good thing. If there's one bad shilling
taken at the grocer's, all the neighbours hear of it, but of

the hundreds of good ones report says nothing. A good woman makes no noise, and no noise is made about her, but a shrew is noted all over the parish. Taking them for all in all, they are most angelical creatures, and a great deal too good for half the husbands.

It is much to the women's credit that there are very few old sayings against husbands, although in this case, sauce for the goose could make capital sauce for the gander; and the mare has as good reasons for kicking as the horse has. They must be very forbearing, or they would have given the men a Roland for every Oliver. Pretty dears, they may be rather quick in their talk, but is it not the nature of bells and belles to have tongues that swing easy? They cannot be so very bad after all, or they would have had their revenge for the many cruel things which are said against them; if they are a bit masterful, their husbands cannot be such very great victims, or they would surely have sense enough to hold their tongues about it. Men don't care to have it known when they are thoroughly well henpecked, and I feel pretty certain that the old sayings are nothing but chaff, for if they were true, men would never dare to admit it.

A true wife is her husband's better half, his lump of delight, his flower of beauty, his guardian angel, and his heart's treasure. He says to her, "I shall in thee most happy be. In thee, my choice, I do rejoice. In thee I find content of mind. God's appointment is my contentment." In her company he finds his earthly heaven; she is the light of his home; the comfort of his soul, and (for this world) the soul of his comfort. Whatever fortune God may send him, he is rich so long as she lives. His rib is the best bone in his body.

The man who weds a loving wife,
Whate'er betideth him in life,
Shall bear up under all;
But he that finds an evil mate,
No good can come within his gate,
His cup is fill'd with gall.

A good husband makes a good wife. Some men can neither do without wives nor with them; they are wretched alone in what is called single blessedness, and they make their homes miserable when they get married; they are like Tompkin's dog, which could not bear to be loose andhowled when it was tied up. Happy bachelors are likely to be happy husbands, and a happy husband is the happiest of men. A well-matched couple carry a joyful life between them, as the two spies carried the cluster of grapes. They are a brace of birds of Paradise. They multiply their joys by sharing them, and lessen their troubles by dividing them: this is fine arithmetic. The wagon of care rolls lightly, along as they pull together, and when it drags a little heavily or there's a hitch anywhere, they love each other all the more, and so lighten the labour.

When a couple fall out, there are always faults on both sides, and generally there is a pound on one and sixteen ounces on the other. When a home is miserable it is as often the husband's fault as the wife's. Darby is as much to blame as Joan, and sometimes more. If the husband won't keep sugar in the cupboard, no wonder his wife gets sour. Want of bread makes want of love; lean dogs fight. Poverty generally rides home on the husband's back, for it is not often the woman's place to go out working for wages. A man down our parts gave his wife a ring with this on it, "If thee don't work, thee shan't eat." He was a brute. It is no business of hers to bring in the flour: she is to see it is well used and not wasted. Therefore, I say, short commons are not her fault. She is not the bread-winner, but the bread-maker. She earns more at home than any wages she can get abroad.

It is not the wife who smokes and drinks away the wages at the "Brown Bear" or the "Jolly Toppers." One sees a drunken woman now and then, and it's an awful sight; but in ninety-nine cases out of a hundred it is the man who comes home tipsy, and abuses the children—the woman seldom does that. The poor drudge of a wife is a teetotaller, whether she likes it or not, and gets plenty of hot water as well as cold. Women are found fault with for often looking into the glass, but that is not so bad a glass as men drown their senses in. The wives do not sit boozing over the taproom-fire; they, poor souls, are shivering at home with the baby, watching the clock (if there is one), wondering when their lords and masters will come home, and crying while they wait. I wonder they don't strike. Some of them are about as wretched as a beetle on a pin or a mouse in a cat's mouth. They have to nurse the sick girl, and wash the dirty boy, and bear with the crying and noise of the children, while his lordship puts on his hat, lights his pipe, and goes off about his own pleasure, or comes in at his own time to find fault with his poor dame for not getting him a fine supper. How could he expect to be fed like a fighting-cock when he brought home so little money on Saturday night and spent so much in worshipping Sir John Barleycorn? I say it, and I know it, there's many a house where there would be no scolding wife if there was not a skulking, guzzling husband. Fellows not fit to be cut up for mops ,drink and drink till all is blue, and then turn on their poor hacks for not having more to give them. Don't tell me, I say it and will maintain it, a woman can't help being vexed when, with all her mending and striving, she can't keep house because her husband won't let her. It would provoke any of us if we had to make bricks without straw, keep the pot boiling without fire, and pay the piper out of an empty purse. What can she get out of the oven when she has neither meal nor dough? You bad husbands, you are thoroughbred sneak and ought to be hung up by your heels till you know better.

They say a man of straw is worth a woman of gold, but I cannot swallow it; a man of straw is worth no more than a woman of straw; let old sayings lie as they like. Jack is no better than Jill, as a rule. When there is wisdom in the husband, there's generally gentleness in the wife, and between them, the old wedding wish is worked out: "One year of joy, another of comfort, and all the rest of content." Where hearts agree, there joy will be. United hearts death only parts. They say *marriage* is not often *merry-age*, but very commonly *mar-age*; well, if so, the coat and waistcoat have as much to do with it as the gown and petticoat. The honeymoon need not come to an end; and when it does, it is often the man's fault for eating all the honey, and leaving nothing but moonshine: when they both agree that whatever becomes of the moon, they will each keep up their share of honey, there's merry living. When a man dwells under the sign of the cat's foot where faces get scratched, either his wife did not marry a man, or he did not marry a woman. If a man cannot take care of himself, his wit must be as scant as the wool of a blue dog. I don't pity most of the men martyrs; I save my pity for the women. When the Dunmow porker is lost, neither of the pair will eat the bacon; but the wife is the most likely to fast for the want of it. Every herring must hang by its own gill, and every person must account for his own share in home quarrels, but John Ploughman can't bear to see all the blame laid on the woman. Whenever a dish is broke, the cat did it, and whenever there is mischief, there's a woman at the bottom of it: here are two as pretty lies as you will meet with in a month's march. There's a "why" for every "wherefore," but the why for family jars does not always lie with the housekeeper. I know some women have long tongues, then the more's the pity that the husbands should set them going; but for the matter of talk just look into a bar-parlour when the men's jaws are well oiled with liquor, and if any woman living can talk faster or be more stupid than the men, my name is not John Ploughman.

When I had got about as far as this, in stepped our minister, and he said, "John, you've got a tough subject, a cut above you; I'll lend you a rare old book to help you over the stile." "Well, sir," said I, "a little help is worth a great deal of faultfinding, and I shall be uncommonly obliged to you."

He sent me down old "Archbishop Secker's Wedding Ring," and a real arch-fellow that Secker was. I could not do any other than pick out some of his pithy bits; they are very flavoury and such as are likely to glue themselves to the memory. He says, "Hast thou a soft heart? It is

"Whenever a dish is broke, the cat did it."

of God's breaking. Hast thou a sweet wife? She is of God's making. The Hebrews have a saying, 'He is not a man that hath not a woman.' Though man alone may be good, yet it is not good that man should be alone. 'Every good gift and every perfect gift is from above.' A wife, though she be not a perfect gift, is a good gift, a beam darted from the Sun of mercy. How happy are those marriages where Christ is at the wedding! Let none but those who have found favour in God's eyes find favour in yours. Husbands should spread a mantle of charity over their wife's infirmities. Do not put out the candle because of the snuff. Husbands and wives should provoke one another to love, and they should love one another notwithstanding provocations. The tree of love should grow up in the midst of the family as the tree of life grew in the garden of Eden. Good servants are a great blessing; good children a greater blessing; and a good wife is the greatest blessing; and such a help let him seek for her that wants one; let him sigh for her that hath lost one; let him delight in her that enjoys one."

To come down from the old Archbishop's roast beef to my own pot herbs, or, as they say, to put Jack after gentleman, I will tell my own experience, and have done.

My experience of my first wife, who will I hope live to be my last, is much as follows: matrimony came from Paradise and leads to it. I never was half so happy before I was a married man as I am now. When you are married your bliss begins. I have no doubt that where there is much love, there will be much to love and where love is scant, faults will be plentiful. If there is only one good wife in England, I am the man who put the ring on her finger, and long may she wear it. God bless the dear soul, if she can put up *with* me, she shall never be put down *by* me.

If I were not married today, and saw a suitable partner, I would be married tomorrow morning before breakfast. What think you of that? "Why," says one, "I think John would get a new wife if he were left a widower." Well, and what if he did, how could he better show that he was happy with his first? I declare I would not say as some do, that they married to have some one to look after the children; I should marry to have some one to look after myself. John Ploughman is a sociable soul, and could not do in a house by himself. One man, when he married his fourth wife, engraved in the ring—

> "If I survive,
> I'll make it five."

What an old Bluebeard!! Marriages are made in heaven: matrimony in itself is good, but there are fools who turn meat into poison, and make a blessing into a curse. "This is a good rope," said Pedley, "I'll hang myself with it." A man who has sought his wife from God and married her for her character, and not merely for her figurehead, may look for a blessing on his choice. They who join their love in God above, who pray to love, and love to pray, will find that love and joy will never cloy.

He who respects his wife will find that she respects him. With what measure he metes it shall be measured to him again, good measure, pressed down, and running over. He who consults his spouse will have a good counsellor. I have heard our minister say, "Women's instincts are often truer than man's reason;" they jump at a thing at once, and are wise offhand. Say what you will of your wife's advice, it's as likely as not you will be sorry you did not take it. He who speaks ill of women should remember the breast he was nursed at, and be ashamed of himself. He who ill treats his wife ought to be whipped at the cart tail, and would not I like a cut at him! I would just brush a fly or two off, trust me for that. So no more at present, as the thatcher said when he had *cleared* every dish on the table.

18
Men with Two Faces

Even bad men praise consistency. Thieves like honest men, for they are the best to rob. When you know where to find a man, he has one good point at any rate; but a fellow who howls with the wolves and bleats with the sheep, gets nobody's good word unless it be the devil's. To carry two faces under one hat is, however, very common. Many roost with the poultry and go shares with Reynard. Many look as if butter would not melt in their mouths, and yet can spit fire when it suits their purpose. I read the other day an advertisement about reversible coats: the tailor who sells them must be making a fortune. Holding with the hare and running with the hounds is still in fashion. Consistency is about as scarce in the world as musk in a dog-kennel.

You may trust some men as far as you can see them, but no further, for new company makes them new men. Like water they boil or freeze, according to the temperature. Some do this because they have no principles; they are of the weathercock persuasion, and turn with the wind. You might as well measure the moon for a suit of clothes as know what they are. They believe in that which pays best. They always put up at the Golden Fleece. Their mill grinds any grist which you bring to it if the ready money is forthcoming; they go with every wind, north, south, east, west, north-east, north-west, south-east, south-west, north-northeast, southwest-by-south, or any other in all the world. Like frogs they can live on land and water, and are not at all particular which it is. Like a cat they always fall on their feet, and will stop anywhere if you butter their toes. They love their friends dearly, but their love lies in the cupboard, and if that be bare, like a mouse, their love runs off to some other larder. They say, "Leave you, dear girl? Never, while you have a shilling." How they scuttle off if you come to the bad! Like rats, they leave a sinking ship.

> When good cheer is lacking,
> Such friends will be packing.

Their heart follows the pudding. While the pot boils they sit by the fire; when the meal tub is empty, they play at turnabout. They believe in the winning horse; they will wear anybody's coat who may choose to give them one; they are to be bought by the dozen, like mackerel, but he who gives a penny for them wastes his money. Profit is their god, and whether they make it out of you or your enemy the money is just as sweet to them. Heads or tails are alike to them so long as they win. High road or back lane, all's the same to them so they can get home with the loaf in the basket. They are friends to the goose, but they will eat his giblets. So long as the water turns their wheel, it is none the worse for being muddy; they would burn their mother's coffin if they were short of firing, and sell their own father if they could turn a penny by the old gentleman's bones. They never lose a chance of minding the main chance.

Others are shifty because they are so desperately fond of good fellowship. "Hail fellow, well met," is their cry, be it traveller or highwayman. They are so good-natured that they must needs agree with everybody. They are cousins of Mr. Anything. Their brains are in other people's heads. If they were at Rome they would kiss the Pope's toe, but when they are at home they make themselves hoarse with shouting, "No Popery." They admire the Vicar of Bray, whose principle was to be the Vicar of Bray whether the Church was Protestant or Popish. They are mere time-servers, in hopes that the times may serve them. They belong to the party which wears the yellow colours not in their button-holes but in the palms of their hands. Butter them, and like turnips you may eat them. Pull the rope, and like the bells they will ring as you choose to make them, funeral knell or wedding peal, come to church or go to the devil. They have no backbones, you may bend them like willow wands, backwards or forwards, whichever way you please. Like oysters, anybody may pepper them who can open them. They are sweet to you and sweet to your enemy. They blow hot and cold. They try to be Jack-o'-both sides and deserve to be kicked like a football by both parties.

Some are hypocrites by nature; slippery as eels, and piebald like Squire Smoothey's mare. Like a drunken man, they could not walk straight if they were to try. Like corndealers, they are rogues in-grain. They wind in and out like a Surrey lane. They are born of the breed of St. Judas. The double shuffle is their favourite game, and honesty their greatest hatred. Honey is on their tongues, but gall in their hearts. They are mongrel bred, like the gypsy's dog. Like a cat's feet, they show soft pads but carry sharp claws. If their teeth are not rotten, their tongues are, and their hearts are like dead men's graves. If speaking the truth and lying were equally profitable,they would naturally prefer to lie, for like dirt to a pig it would be congenial. They fawn, and flatter, and cringe, and scrape, for like snails they make their way by their slime; but all the while they hate you in their hearts, and only wait for a chance to stab you. Beware of those who come from the town of deceit. Mr. Facing-both-ways, Mr. Fair-speech, and Mr. Two-tongues are neighbours who are best at a distance. Though they look one way, as boatmen do, they are pulling the other; they are false as the devil's promises, and as cruel as death and the grave.

Religious deceivers are the worst of vermin, and I fear they are as plentiful as rats in an old wheat stack.

"They are like a silver pin,
Fair without but foul within."

They cover up their black flesh with white feathers. Saturday and Sunday make a wonderful difference in them. They have the fear of the minister a deal more before their eyes than the fear of God. Their religion lies in imitating the religious; they have none of the root of the matter in them. They carry Dr. Watts' hymn book in their pocket, and sing a roaring song at the same time. Their Sunday coats are the best part about them; the nearer you get to their hearts the more filth you will find. They prate like parrots, but their talk and their walk do not agree. Some of them are fishing for customers, and a little pious talk is a cheap advertisement; and if the seat at the church or the meeting costs a trifle they make it up out of short weights. They don't worship God while they trade, but they trade on their worship. Others of the poorer sort go to church for soup, and bread, and coal tickets. They love the communion because of the alms' money. Some of the dear old Mrs. Goodbodies want a blessed almshouse, and so they profess to be so blessed under the blessed ministry of their blessed pastor every blessed Sabbath. Charity suits them if faith does not; they know which side their bread is buttered on.

Others make a decent show in religion to quiet their consciences; they use it as a salve for their wounds—and if they could satisfy heaven as easily as they quiet themselves, it would be a fine thing for them. It has been my lot to meet with some who went a long way in profession, as far as I could see, for nothing but the love of being thought a deal of. They got a little knot of friends to believe in their fine talk, and take all in for gospel that they liked to say. Their opinion was the true measure of a preacher's soundness; they could settle up everything by their own know, and they had gallons of XXX experience for those who liked something hot and strong; but dear, dear, if they had but condescended to show a little Christian practice as well, how much better their lives would have weighed up! These people are like owls, which look to be big birds, but they are not, for they are all feathers; and they look wonderfully knowing in the twilight, but when the light comes they are regular boobies.

Hypocrites of all sorts are abominable, and he who deals with them will rue it. He who tries to cheat the Lord will be quite ready to cheat his fellow men. Great cry generally means little wool. Many a big chimney in which you expect to see bacon and hams, when you look up it, has nothing to show you but its empty hooks and black soot. Some men's windmills are only nut-crackers—their elephants are nothing but sucking-pigs. It is not all who go to church or meeting that truly pray, nor those who sing loudest that praise God most, nor those who pull the longest faces who are the most in earnest.

What mean animals hypocrites must be! Talk of polecats and weasels, they are nothing to them. Better be a dead dog than a live hypocrite. Surely when the devil sees hypocrites at their little game it must be as good as a play to him; he tempts genuine Christians, but he lets these alone, because he is sure of them. He need not shoot at lame ducks, his dog can pick them up any day.

Depend upon it, friends, if a straight line will not pay, a crooked one won't. What is got by shuffling is very dangerous gain. It may give a moment's peace to wear a mask, but deception will come home to you and bring sorrow with it. Honesty is the best policy. If the lion's skin does not do, never try the fox's. Be as true as steel. Let your face and hands, like the church clock, always tell how your inner works are going. Better be laughed at as Tom Tell-truth than be praised as Crafty Charlie. Plain dealing may bring us trouble, but it is better than shuffling. At the last, the upright will have their reward, but for the double-minded to get to heaven is as impossible as for a man to swim across the Atlantic with a millstone under each arm.

19
Hints As To Thriving

Hard work is the grand secret of success. Nothing but rags and poverty can come of idleness. Elbow grease is the only stuff to make gold with. No sweat no sweet. He who would have the crow's eggs must climb the tree. Every man must build up his own fortune nowadays. Shirt sleeves rolled up lead on to best broadcloth; and he who is not ashamed of the apron will soon be able to do without it. "Diligence is the mother of good luck," as poor Richard says; but "Idleness is the devil's bolster," as John Ploughman says.

Believe in travelling on step by step; don't expect to be rich in a jump.

> Great greediness to reap,
> Helps not the money heap.

Slow and sure is better than fast and flimsy. Perseverance, by its daily gains, enriches a man far more than fits and starts of fortunate speculation. Little fishes are sweet. Every little helps, as the sow said when she snapped at a gnat. Every day a thread makes a skein in a year. Brick by brick houses are built. We should creep before we walk, walk before we run, and run before we ride. In getting rich, the more haste the worse speed. Haste trips up its own heels. Hasty climbers have sudden falls.

It is bad beginning business without capital. It is hard marketing with empty pockets. We want a nest egg, for hens will lay where there are eggs already. It is true you must bake with the flour you have, but if the sack is empty it might be quite as well not to set up for a baker. Making bricks without straw is easy enough compared with making money when you have none to start with. You, young gentleman, stay as a journeyman a little longer till you have saved a few pounds; fly when your wings have got feathers; but if you try it too soon you will be like the young rook that broke its neck through trying to fly before it was fledged. Every minnow wants to be a whale, but it is prudent to be a little fish while you have but little water; when your pond becomes the sea, then swell as much as you like. Trading without capital is like building a house without bricks, making a fire without sticks, burning candles without wicks; it leads men into tricks, and lands them in a fix.

Don't give up a small business till you see that a large one will pay you better. Even crumbs are bread.

> Better a poor horse than an empty stall;
> Better half a loaf than none at all.

Better a little furniture than an empty house. In these hard times he who can sit on a stone and feed himself had better not move. From bad to worse is poor improvement. A crust is hard fare, but none at all is harder. Don't jump out of the frying pan into the fire. Remember, many men have done well in very small shops. A little trade with profit is better than a great concern at a loss; a small fire that warms you is better than a large fire that burns you. A great deal of water can be got from a small pipe if the bucket is always there to catch it. Large hares may be caught in small woods. A sheep may get fat in a small meadow, and starve in a great desert. He who undertakes too much succeeds but little. Two shops are like two stools, a man comes to the ground between them. You may burst a bag by trying to fill it too full, and ruin yourself by grasping at too much.

> In a great river great fish are found,
> But take good heed lest you be drown'd.

Make as few changes as you can; trees often transplanted bear little fruit. If you have difficulties in one place you will have them in another; if you move because it is damp in the valley, you may find it cold on the hill. Where; will the ass go that he will not have to work? Where can a cow live and not get milked? Where will you find land without stones or meat without bones? Everywhere on earth men must eat bread in the sweat of their faces. To fly from trouble, men must have eagles' wings. Alteration is not always improvement, as the pigeon said when she got out of the net and into the pie. There is a proper time for changing, and then mind you bestir yourself, for a sitting hen gets no barley. But do not be forever on the shift, for a rolling stone gathers no moss. stick-to-it is the conqueror. He who can wait long enough will win. This, that, and the other, anything, and everything, all put together make nothing in the end; but on one horse a man rides home in due season. In one place the seed grows; in one nest the bird hatches its eggs; in one oven the bread bakes; in one river the fish lives.

Do not be above your business. He who turns up his nose at his work quarrels with his bread and butter. He is a poor smith who is afraid of his own sparks; there's some discomfort in all trades except chimney-sweeping. If sailors gave up going to sea because of the wet; if bakers left off baking because it was hot work; if ploughmen would not plough because of the cold, and tailors would not make our clothes for fear of pricking their fingers, what a pass we should come to! Nonsense, my fine fellow, there's no shame about any honest calling; don't be afraid of soiling your hands, there's plenty of soap to be had. All trades are good to good traders. A clever man can make money out of dirt. Lucifer matches pay well if you sell enough of them.

> Never mind the stink,
> Sweet smells the chink.

You cannot get honey if you are frightened of bees, nor sow corn if you are afraid of getting mud on your boots. Lackadaisical gentlemen had better emigrate to Fool's-land, where men get their living by wearing shiny boots and lavender gloves. When bars of iron melt under the south wind, when you can dig the fields with tooth-picks, blow ships along with fans, manure the crops with lavender water, and grow plumcake in flower pots, then will be a fine time for dandies; but until the millennium comes, we shall all have a deal to put up with and had better bear our present burdens than run helter-skelter where we shall find matters a deal worse.

Plod is the word. Everyone must row with such oars as he has, and as he can't choose the wind, he must sail by such as God sends him. Patience and attention will get on in the long run. If the cat sits long enough at the hole she will catch the mouse. Always at it grows good cabbage and lettuce where others grow thistles. I know as a ploughman that it is up and down, up and down the field that ploughs the acres; there's no getting over the ground by a mile at a time. He who plods on the clods, rods on rods will turn of the sods while laziness nods.

Keep your weather eye open. Sleeping poultry are carried off by the fox. Who watches not catches not. Fools ask what's o' clock, but wise men know their time. Grind while the wind blows, or if not do not blame providence. God sends every bird its food, but He does not throw it into the nest; He gives us our daily bread, but it is through our own labour. Take time by the forelock. Be up early and catch the worm. The morning hour carries gold in its mouth. He who drives last in the row gets all the dust in his eyes; rise early, and you will have a clear start for the day.

Never try dirty dodges to make money. It will never pay you to lick honey off of thorns. An honest man will not make a dog of himself for the sake of getting a bone. It is hard to walk on the devil's ice; it is fine skating, but it ends in a heavy fall and worse. He needs have a long spoon who would eat out of the same dish with Satan. Never ruin your soul for the sake of money: it is like drowning yourself in a well to get a drink of water. Take nothing in hand that may bring you repentance. Better walk barefoot than ride in a carriage to hell; better that the bird starve than be fattened for the spit. The mouse wins little by nibbling the cheese if it gets caught in the trap. Clean money or none, mark that; for gain badly got will be an everlasting loss.

A good article, full weight, and a fair price bring customers to the shop, but people do not recommend the shop where they are cheated. Cheats never thrive; or if they do it must be in London, where they catch chance customers enough to live by. The long-bow man may hit the mark sometimes, but a fair shot is the best. A rogue's purse is full of holes. He will have blisters on his feet who wears stolen shoes. He whose fingers are like lime-twigs will find other things stick to them besides silver. Steal eels and they will turn to snakes. The more a fox robs the sooner he will be hunted. If a rogue wants to make a good trade he had better turn honest. If all you aim at is profit, still deal uprightly, for it is the most paying game.

Look most to your spending. No matter what comes in, if more goes out you will always be poor. The art is not in making money, but in keeping it; little expenses, like mice in a barn, when they are many, make great waste. Hair by hair heads get bald; straw by straw the thatch goes off the cottage, and drop by drop the rain comes into the chamber. A barrel is soon empty if the tap leaks but a drop a minute. Chickens will be plucked feather by feather if the maid keeps at it; small mites eat the cheese; little birds destroy a great deal of wheat. When you mean to save, begin with your mouth; there are many thieves down the red lane. The ale jug is a great waster. In all other things, keep within compass. In clothes, choose suitable and lasting stuff, and not tawdry fineries. To be warm is the main thing; never mind the looks. Never stretch your legs further than your blankets will reach, or you will soon be cold. A fool may make money, but it needs a wise man to spend it. Remember it is easier to build two chimneys than to keep one going. If you give all to room and board, there is nothing left for the savings bank. Fare hard and work hard while you are young, and you have a chance of rest when you are old.

Never indulge in extravagances unless you want to make a short cut to the workhouse. Money has wings of its own, and if you find it another pair of wings, wonder not if it flies fast.

> He that hath it, and will not keep it;
> He that wants it, and will not seek it;
> He that drinks and is not dry,
> Shall want money as well as I.

If our poor people could only see the amount of money which they melt away in drink, their hair would stand on end with fright. Why, they swallow rivers of beer, seas of porter, and great big lakes of spirits and other fire waters. We should all be clothed like gentlemen and live like fighting cocks if what is wasted on booze could be sensibly used. We would need to get up earlier in the morning to spend all our money, for we would find ourselves suddenly made quite rich, and all that through stopping the drip of the tap. At any rate, you young people who want to get on in the world must make a point of dropping your half-pints and settle in your spirits that no spirits shall ever settle you. Have your luxuries, if you must have them, after you have made your fortunes, but just now look after your bread and cheese.

Pray excuse me for spinning this long yarn, for as I pulled, it came. My talk seems like the Irishman's rope which he could not get into the ship because somebody had cut the end off. I only want to say, do not be greedy, for covetousness is always poor; still strive to get on, for poverty is no virtue, and to rise in the world is to a man's credit as well as his comfort. Earn all you can, save all you can, and then give all you can. Never try to save out of God's cause; such money will canker the rest. Giving to God is no loss; it is putting your substance into the best bank. Giving is true having, as the old gravestone said of the dead man, "What I spent I had, what I saved I lost, what I gave I have." The pockets of the poor are safe lockers, and it is always a good investment to lend to the Lord. John Ploughman wishes all young beginners long life and prosperity.

> Sufficient of wealth,
> And abundant health,
> Long years of content,
> And when life is spent,
> A mansion with God in glory.

20
Tall Talk

The art of stretching is uncommonly general nowadays. Gooseberries are to be heard of weighing twice as much as possible, and unseen showers of frogs fall regularly when newspapers are slack. If a cart goes by, and rattles the lid of an old woman's teapot, it is at once put down as an earthquake. Fine imaginations are not at all scarce.

Certain people are always on the look out for wonders, and if they don't see them they invent them. They see comets every night, and hear some rare tale every day. All their molehills are mountains. All their ducks are swans. They have learned the multiplication table, and use it freely. If they saw six dogs together they would swear they saw a hundred hounds; yes, and get as red in the face as turkey-cocks if anybody looked a little doubtful; and before long they would persuade themselves that they saw ten thousand lions; for everything grows with them as fast as mushrooms, and as big as Box Hill.

All things around them are wonderful, but as for themselves, nobody is fit to clean their boots. They are the cream of creation. They are as strong as Samson, and could pull against John Ploughman's team, only they won't try it, for fear of hurting the horses. Their wealth is enormous; they *could* pay off the National Debt, only they have good reasons for not doing so just yet. If they keep shop they turn over several millions in the year, and only stop in business at all for the sake of their neighbours. They sell the best goods at the lowest prices, in fact, under cost price none in the county is fit to hold a candle to them; their business is cock of the walk and king of the castle. If they take a farm it is only for amusement, and to show the poor ignorant natives how to do it. All their doings are wonders! Like the wild beast show which stopped at our village the other day, they are *the only, original, and unrivalled!* But they are quite as dead a sell as that fine affair was; all the best of it was outside on the pictures, and it's just the same with them. But, bless you, how they do draw the long bow! Hear them talk. It is all in capital letters and notes of admiration. "Did you ever see SUCH A NAG? Why, sir, it would beat the wind! THAT COW—let me call your attention to her, there is not such another in the county; JUST NOTICE THE SWING OF HER TAIL!! Yes, sir, THAT BOY of mine *is* intelligent, far beyond his years. He's a perfect prodigy! *Like his father*, did you say? Very kind remark, sir, but there's a good deal of truth in it: though I say it, a man must get up early to beat ME! *I'm one too many for most people!* Just look over the farm, sir. Was there ever such A FIELD OF TURNIPS? The fly on the leaf? Not a bit, sir; that arises from the peculiar sort; it's A VERY RARE TURNIP, with ventilated leaves pricked through by nature to let the air in and out! Too many moles did you say? Ah! thereby hangs a tale. Do you know OUR MOLES are a great singularity? They throw up bigger

"Though I say it, a man must get up early to beat me."

hills than any others in England, and are supposed to be of a FINE OLD BRITISH STOCK now almost lost. Did you notice that TREMENDOUS THISTLE? Is it not a rare specimen? Enough to make a Scotchman die of joy. That shows the EXTRAORDINARY richness of the soil; and, indeed, sir, OUR LAST YEAR'S CROP OF WHEAT was so amazingly heavy, I thought we should never get it home; it nearly broke the wagons; we had half the county here to see it threshed, and the oldest men in the parish said they never heard tell of the like. IT IS A MERCY THAT STEAM IS INVENTED, OR WE NEVER COULD HAVE THRESHED IT BY HAND."

When a man gets into this style of talk, it is no matter what he is hammering at, he speaks of it as the finest, greatest, and most marvellous in the kingdom, or else the most awful, horrible, and dreadful in the world. His boots would not fit Goliath but his tongue is much too big for the giant's mouth. He paints with a broom. He sugars his dumpling with a spade, and lays on his butter with a trowel. *His* horse, *his* dog, *his* gun, *his* wife, *his* child, *his* singing, *his* planning, are all without equal; he is the pillar of the parish, he lives at Number One, and it would be hard to find a man fit to be number two to him. The water out of his well is stronger than wine; it rains pea-soup into his cistern; his currant bushes grow grapes; you might live inside one of his pumpkins; and his flowers— well, he's heard that the Queen herself had the fellow plant to that geranium, only his was rather the better! The greatest wonder is that men of this kidney don't see that everybody is laughing at them; they must have bragged themselves blind. Everybody sees the bottom of their dish, and yet they go on calling it an ocean, as if they had none but flat fish to deal with.

I've known men who open their mouths like barn doors in boasting what they would do *if* they were in somebody else's shoes. If they were in Parliament they would abolish all taxes, turn workhouses into palaces, make the pumps run with beer, and set the Thames on fire; but all this depends on an *if*, and that *if* is a sort of five-barred gate which they have never got over. If the sky falls we shall catch larks. If Jack Brag does but get the reins he'll make the horses fly up to the moon. *If* is a fine word; when a man jumps on its back it will carry him into worlds which were never created, and make him see miracles which were never wrought. With an if you may put all London into a quart pot.

> "If all the seas were one sea,
> What a great sea that would be!
> And if all the trees were one tree,
> What a great tree that would be!
> And if all the axes were one axe,
> What a great axe that would be!
> And if all the men were one man,
> What a great man he would be!
> And if the great man took the great axe,
> And cut down the great tree,
> And let it fall into the great sea,
> What a splish splash that would be!"

"What nonsense!" says one; so John Ploughman thinks, and therefore he puts it in as a specimen of the stupidity which tall talkers are so fond of. This is not half so silly as nine out of ten of their mighty nothings.

What some of these fellows have done! Now, would you believe it? (I say, "No, I would not.") They made their own fortunes in no time, and made other people's, too. Their advice has been the means of filling many a bag with gold. What they said at a meeting fastened the people to their seats like a cobbler's wax. They were in a quarrel, and when all their party were nearly beaten, they settled off the opposition side at once with first-rate wit and wisdom—King Solomon was a fool to them. As to religion, they were the first to set it up in the parish, and by their wonderful exertions, everything was set a going. They laid the golden egg. People are not grateful, or they would almost worship them: it's shameful to see how they have been neglected, and even turned off of late by the very people whom they have been the making of. While they had a finger in the pie all went well at the meeting, but now they have left they say there's a screw loose, and they who live longest will see most. When they are in a modest humour, they borrow words from David and say, "The earth is dissolved, I bear up the pillars of it." It is thought that their death would fill the world with bones. If they remove their custom people are expected to shut up their shops directly, and it is only their impudence that makes them hope to get a living after such customers are gone. When they feel a little natural pride at their great doings, then it's fine to hear them go ahead: talk of blowing your own trumpet, they have a whole band of music, big drum and all, and keep all the instruments going first-rate to their own praise and glory.

I'd rather plough all day and be on the road with the wagon all night when it freezes your eyelashes off, than listen to those great talkers; they make me as sick as a cat. I'd sooner go without eating till I was as lean as wash-leather, than eat the best turkey that ever came on the table, and be dinned all the while with their awful jaw. They talk on such a mighty big scale, and magnify everything so thunderingly, that you cannot believe them when they accidentally slip in a word or two of truth; and so you are apt to think that even their cheese is chalk. They are great liars, but they are hardly conscious of it; they have talked themselves into believing their own bombast. The frog thought herself equal to the cow, and then began to blow herself out to make it true; they swell like her and they will burst like her if they don't mind.

Everybody who knows these big talkers should take warning from them:

> Said I to myself, here's a lesson for me,
> This man is a picture of what I might be.

We must try to state the truth, the whole truth, and nothing but the truth. If we begin calling eleven inches a foot we shall go on till we call one inch four-and-twenty. If we call a heifer a cow, we may one day call a dormouse a bullock. Once go in for exaggeration, and you may as well be hung for a sheep as a lamb. You have left the road of truth, and there is no telling where the crooked lane may lead you to. He who tells little lies, will soon think nothing of great ones, for the principle is the same. Where there is a mouse-hole, there will soon be a rat-hole; and if the kitten comes the cat will follow. It seldom rains but it pours, a little untruth leads on to a perfect shower of lying.

Self-praise is no recommendation. A man's praise smells sweet when it comes out of other men's mouths, but in his own it stinks. Grow your own cherries, but don't sing your own praises.

Boasters are never worth a button with the shank off. Long tongue, short hand. Great talkers, little doers. Dogs that bark much run away when it is time to bite. The leanest pig squeaks most. It is not the hen which cackles most that lays most eggs. Saying and doing are two different things. It is the barren cow that bellows. There may be great noise of threshing where there is no wheat. Great boast, little roast. Much froth, little beer. Drums sound loud because there is nothing in them. Good men know themselves too well to chant their own praises. Barges without cargoes float high on the canal, but the fuller they are the lower they sink. Good cheese sells itself without puffery; good wine needs no bush; and when men are really excellent, people find it out without telling. Bounce is the sign of folly. Loud braying reveals an ass. If a man is ignorant and holds his tongue, no one will despise him; but if he rattles on with an empty pate, and a tongue that brags like forty, he will write out his own name in capital letters, and they will be these—F, O, O, L.

As "by the ears the ass is known"—
A truth as sure as parsons preach,
"The man" as proverbs long have shown,
"Is seen most plainly through his speech."

21
Things I Would Not Choose

If it were all the same to other folks and I might have things managed exactly as I liked, I should not choose to have my homely book pulled to pieces by fellows who have not the honesty to read it, but make up their minds beforehand, as Simple Simon did when they put him on the jury. However, as the rhinoceros said, I have not a very thin skin; and if it amuses others to find fault with me they are as welcome as they are free. The anvil is not afraid of the hammer.

They tell me those London editors cut a page open, and then smell the knife, and fall to praising the book up to the skies, or abusing it without mercy, according as the maggot bites them, or according to what they have had for dinner. John Ploughman hopes the publisher will turn down this leaf when he sends his book to the papers, and he hopes the following word to the wise will be enough: *I hope my pears won't fall into pigs' mouths.*

I should not choose, if I might have my own way, to see a dozen of these pages brought home wrapped round the butter the next time we send to the shop; but it is not at all unlikely to happen, so I must put up with it, as Tom Higgs did when he had only turkey and plum pudding for dinner.

I should not choose to plough with two old horses spavined and broken-winded and altogether past work: pity the poor horses and pity the poor ploughman, and no pity at all for the farmer who keeps such wretched cattle. When I see a man whipping and slashing a poor brute of a horse, I want to kick him, but at the same time, I feel glad that Violet and Dapper go well enough with the sound of the whip without needing to be paid like lawyers for all they do. A man who knocks a horse about ought to be put in harness himself, and be driven about by a butcher. There's a deal to be done with animals with kindness, and nothing with cruelty. He who is unmerciful to his beast is worse than a beast himself.

I should not choose to be a bob-tailed cow in summertime, nor a servant with a score of masters, nor a minister with half-a-dozen ignorant tyrants for deacons, nor a man who lives with his mother-in-law. Nor should I like to try the truth of the old saying:—

> "Two cats and one mouse,
> Two women in one house,
> Two dogs to one bone,
> Will not agree long."

I had rather not be a dog with a tin kettle tied to his tail, nor a worm on a fisherman's hook, nor an eel being skinned alive, nor a husband with a vixen for his wife. I would much rather not fall into the jaws of a crocodile or the hands of a lawyer: the only suit that lasts too long is a lawsuit, and that would not suit me at all. I would not choose to be gossiped to death by wild washerwomen, or pestered by a travelling bookseller wanting me to take in sixpenny numbers of a book that will run on forever like old Jimmy's debts.

I should be very hard up before I should choose to sleep with pigs, or live in some people's dirty houses. I would not choose to own half the cottages poor labourers are made to live in: no farmer would be so mean as to keep his horses in them; and they are not good enough for dog kennels. Think of father, and mother, and a grown-up son, and two daughters sleeping in the same room! It is a burning shame and a crying sin on the part of those who drive people to such shifts. It won't bear to be thought of, and yet it is not at all uncommon. Squires and landlords, how would you like it? If any man defends such a system half-an-hour's hanging would be a good thing for him.

To be servant to a miser, to work for a wasp, to be cats paw to a monkey, or toady to a lord without brains, I would not choose; nor to go to the workhouse, nor apply for parish relief; I'd sooner try Grantham gruel, nine grits and a gallon of water. I would not go round with the hat for my own pocket, nor borrow money, nor be a loafer, nor live like a toad under a harrow; no, not for all that ever thawed out of the cold hand of charity.

Bad off as I am, I would not choose to change, unless I could hope to better myself. Who would go under the spout to get out of the rain? What's the use of travelling to the other end of the world to be worse off than you are? Old England for me, and Botany Bay for those who like to transport themselves.

I would not choose to drive a pig, nor to manage a jibbing nag, nor try to persuade a man with a wooden head; nor should I like to be a schoolmaster with unruly boys, nor a bull baited by dogs, nor a hen who has hatched ducks. Worse off still is a preacher to drowsy hearers; he hunts with dead dogs and drives wooden horses. As well hold a service for sleeping swine as sleeping men.

I would not buy a horse of a horse dealer if I could help it, for the two or three honest ones nobody ever heard of. A very honest horse dealer will never cheat you if you don't let him; an ordinary one will draw your eye-tooth while your mouth is shut. Horses are almost as hard to judge of as men's hearts; the oldest hands are taken in. What with bone-spavin, ringbone and splints; grease, crown-scab and rat-tail, wind-galls and cankers, colic and jaundice, sandcracks and founders, mallenders and sallenders, there is hardly a sound horse in the world. It's a bad thing to change horses at all; if you have a good one keep it, for you will not get a better; if you have a bad one keep it, for ten to one you will buy a worse.

I would not choose to make myself a doormat nor a poodle, nor a fellow who will eat dirt in order to curry favour with great folks. Let who will tell lies to please others, I'd rather have truth on my side, if I go barefoot. Independence and a clear conscience are better with cold cabbage than slavery and sin with roast beef.

I would not like to keep a toll-gate at the top of a long hill, nor to be a tax-collector, nor the summoning officer, nor a general nuisance, nor a poor postman with half enough to live on and twice as much to do as he ought; better to be a gypsy's horse, and live on the common with no hay and no oats but plenty of oak cudgel.

I would not choose to be plucked like a goose, nor to be shareholder in a company, nor to be fried alive, nor to be at the mercy of a Roman Catholic priest. I would not stand as godfather to anybody's child, to promise that the little sinner shall keep God's holy commandments and walk in the same all the days of his life. Of the two, I would sooner promise to put the moon into my coat sleeve and bring it out again at the leg of my trousers, or vow that the little dear shall have red hair and a snub nose. Neither would I choose to have lies told over my baby in the hope of getting on the parson's blind side when the blankets were given away at Christmas.

I would not choose to go where I should be afraid to die, nor could I bear to live without a good hope for hereafter. I would not choose to sit on a barrel of gunpowder and smoke a pipe, but that is what those do who are thoughtless about their souls while life is so uncertain. Neither would I choose my lot on earth, but leave it with God to choose for me. I might pick and choose, and take the worst, but His choice is always best.

22
Try

Of all the pretty little songs I have ever heard my youngsters sing, that is one of the best which winds up—

"If at first you don't succeed,
Try, try, try again."

I recommend it to grown up people who are down in the mouth, and fancy that the best thing they can do is to give up. Nobody knows what he can do till he tries. "We shall get through it now," said Jack to Harry as they finished up the pudding. Everything new is hard work, but a little of the "TRY" ointment rubbed on the hand and worked into the heart makes all things easy.

Can't do it sticks in the mud, but Try soon drags the wagon out of the rut. The fox said Try, and he got away from the hounds when they almost snapped at him. The bees said Try, and turned flowers into honey. The squirrel said Try, and up he went to the top of the beech tree. The snowdrop said Try, and bloomed in the cold snows of winter. The sun said Try, and the spring soon threw Jack Frost out of the saddle. The young lark said Try, and he found that his new wings took him over hedges and ditches, and up where his father was singing. The ox said

Try, and ploughed the field from end to end. No hill too steep for Try to climb, no clay too stiff for Try to plough, no field too wet for Try to drain, no hole too big for Try to mend.

> "By little strokes,
> Men fell great oaks."

By a spadeful at a time the navvies digged the cutting, cut a big hole through the hill, and heaped up the embankment.

> "The stone is hard, and the drop is small,
> But a hole is made by the constant fall."

What man has done man can do, and what has never been, may be. Ploughmen have got to be gentlemen, cobblers have turned their lapstones into gold, and tailors have sprouted into members of Parliament. Tuck up your shirt-sleeves, young Hopeful, and go at it. Where there's a will there's a way. The sun shines for all the world. Believe in God, and stick to hard work, and see if the mountains are not removed. Faint heart never won fair lady. Cheer, boys, cheer, God helps those who help themselves. Never mind luck, that's what the fool had when he killed himself with eating suet pudding; the best luck in all the world is made up of joint oil and sticking plaster.

Don't wait for helpers. Try those two old friends, your strong arms. Self's the man. If the fox wants poultry for his cubs he must carry the chickens home himself. None of her friends can help the hare; she must run for herself, or the greyhounds will have her. Every man must carry his own sack to the mill. You must put your own shoulder to the wheel and keep it there, for there's plenty of ruts in the road. If you wait till all the ways are paved, you will have the light shining between your ribs. If you sit there till great men take you on their backs, you will grow to your seat. Your own legs are better than stilts; don't look to others, but trust in God and keep your powder dry.

Don't be whining about not having a fair start. Throw a sensible man out of a window, he'll fall on his legs and ask the nearest way to his work. The more you have to begin with the less you will have at the end. Money you earn yourself is much brighter and sweeter than any you get out of dead men's bags. A scant breakfast in the morning of life whets the appetite for a feast later in the day. He who has tasted a sour apple will have the more relish for a sweet one; your present want will make future prosperity all the sweeter. Eighteenpence has set up many a pedlar in business, and he has turned it over till he has kept his carriage.

As for the place you are cast in, don't find fault with that. You need not be a horse because you were born in a stable. If a bull tossed a man of mettle sky high he would drop down into a good place. A hard-working young man, with his wits about him, will make money where others do nothing but lose it.

> "Who loves his work and knows to spare,
> May live and flourish anywhere."

As to a little trouble, who expects to find cherries without stones, or roses without thorns? Who would win must learn to bear. Idleness lies in bed sick of the mulligrubs, where industry finds health and wealth. The dog in the kennel barks at the fleas; the hunting dog does not even know they are there. Laziness waits till the river is dry and never gets to market; "Try" swims it and makes all the trade. Can't do it couldn't eat the bread and butter which was cut for him, but Try made meat out of mushrooms.

Everybody who does not get on lays it all on competition. When the wine was stolen they said it was the rats; it's very convenient to have a horse to put the saddle on. A mouse may find a hole, be the room ever so full of cats. Good workmen are always wanted. There's a penny to be turned at the worst booth in the fair. No barber ever shaves so close but another barber will find something left. Nothing is so good but what it might be better; and he who sells the best wins the trade. We were all going to the workhouse because of the new machines, so the prophets down at the taproom were always telling us; but instead of it, all these threshing, and reaping, and hay-making machines have helped to make those men better off who had sense enough to work them. If a man has not a soul above clod-hopping he may expect to keep poor, but if he opens his sense-box and picks up here a little and there a little, even Johnny Raw may yet improve. "Times are bad," they say; yes, and if you go gaping about and send your wits woolgathering, times always will be bad.

Many don't get on because they have not the pluck to begin in right earnest. The first pound laid by is the difficulty. The first blow is half the battle. Over with that beer jug, up with the "Try" flag, then out to your work and away to the savings bank with the savings, and you will be a man yet. Poor men will always be poor if they think they must be. But there's a way up out of the lowest poverty if a man looks after it early, before he has a wife and half-a-dozen children: after that he carries too much weight for racing, and most commonly he must be content if he finds bread for the hungry mouths and clothes for the little backs. Yet, I don't know; some hens scratch all the better for having a great swarm of chicks. To young men the road up the hill may be hard, but at any rate it is open and they who set stout hearts against a stiff hill shall climb it yet. What was hard to bear will be sweet to remember. If young men would deny themselves, work hard, live hard, and save in their early days, they need not keep their noses to the grindstone all their lives, as many do. Let them be teetotalers for economy's sake; water is the strongest drink, it drives mills. It's the drink of lions and horses, and Samson never drank anything else. The beer money would soon build a house.

If you want to do good in the world, the little word "Try" comes in again. There are plenty of ways of serving God, and some that will fit you exactly as a key fits a lock. Don't hold back because you cannot preach in St. Paul's; be content to talk to one or two in a cottage; very good wheat grows in little fields. You may cook in small pots as well as in big ones. Little pigeons can carry great messages. Even a little dog can bark at a thief, and wake up the master, and save the house. A spark is fire. A sentence of truth has heaven in it. Do what you do right thoroughly, pray over it heartily, and leave the result to God.

Alas! Advice is thrown away on many, like good seed on a bare rock. Teach a cow for seven years, but she will never learn to sing the Old Hundredth. Of some it seems

"Even a little dog can bark at a thief and save the house."

true that when they were born, Solomon went by the door but would not look in. Their coat of arms is a fool's cap on a donkey's head. They sleep when it is time to plough and weep when harvest comes. They eat all the parsnips for supper and wonder they have none left for breakfast. Our working people are shamefully unthrifty, and soold England swarms with poor. If what goes into the mash-tub went into the kneading-trough, families would be better fed and better taught. If what is spent in waste were only saved against a rainy day, workhouses would never be built.

> Once let every man say *Try*,
> Very few on straw would lie,
> Fewer still of want would die;
> Pans would all have fish to fry;
> Pigs would fill the poor man's sty;
> Want would cease and need would fly;
> Wives and children cease to cry;
> Poor rates would not swell so high;
> Things wouldn't go so much awry—
> You'd be glad, and so would I.

23
Monuments

Every man should leave a monument behind him in the recollection of his life by his neighbours. There's something very much amiss about a man who is not missed when he dies. A good character is the best tombstone. Those who loved you, and were helped by you, will remember you when forget-me-nots are withered. Carve your name on hearts, and not on marble. So live towards others that they will keep you; memory green when the grass grows on your grave. Let us hope there will be something better to be said about us than of the man whose epitaph is—

> "Here lies a man who did no good,
> And if he'd lived he never would;
> Where he's gone, and how he fares,
> Nobody knows and nobody cares."

May our friends never remember us as great gormandizers of meat and drink, like the glutton over whose grave is written—

> "Gentle reader, gentle reader,
> Look on the spot where I do lie,
> I was always a very good feeder,
> But now the worms do feed on I."

As much as that might be said of a prize pig or a fat bullock if it died of disease. Some men are nothing better than walking beer barrels while they live; when death staves in the cask, they deserve to rot out of notice.

However, a plain-speaking tombstone is better than downright lying. To put flattery on a grave is like pouring melted butter down a stone sink. What queer tastes those must have who puff off the departed, as if they wanted to blow the trumpet of the dead before the last angel makes his appearance! Here's an apple out of their basket—

> "Here lies the body of Martha Gwyn,
> Who was so very pure within;
> She crack'd the outer shell of sin,
> And hatch'd herself a cherubim."

Where do they bury the bad people? Right and left in our churchyard they seem all to have been the best of folks, a regular nest of saints; and some of them so precious good, it is no wonder they died—they were too fine to live in such a wicked world as this. Better give bread to the poor than stones to the dead. Better kind words to the living than fine speeches over the grave. Some of the fulsome stuff on monuments is enough to make a dead man blush.

What heaps of marble are stuck over many big people's tombs! Half enough to build a house with! What a lift they will have at the resurrection! It makes me feel as if I could not get my breath to think of all those stones being heaped on my bones; not that there's any fear of it. Let the earth which I have turned over so often lie light upon my corpse when it is turned over me. Let John

Ploughman be buried somewhere under the boughs of a spreading beech, with a green grass mound above him, out of which primroses and daisies keep in their season; a quiet shady spot where the leaves fall, and the robins play, and the dewdrops gleam in the sunshine. Let the wind blow fresh and free over my grave, and if there must be a line about me, let it be—

HERE LIES THE BODY OF
JOHN PLOUGHMAN
WAITING FOR THE APPEARING OF HIS
LORD AND SAVIOUR
JESUS CHRIST.

I've often heard tell of patience on a monument, but I have never seen it sitting there when I have gone through churchyards; I have a good many times seen stupidity on a monument, and I have wondered why the parson, or the churchwarden, or the beadle, or whoever else has the ruling of things, let people cut such rubbish on the stones. Why, a Glos'tershire man told me that at Dymock graveyard there's a writing like this:

> "Two sweeter babes you nare did see—
> Than God amity gave to wee;
> But they wur ortaken wee agur fits,
> And hear they lys has as dead as nits."

I've read pretty near enough silly things myself in our Surrey burying grounds to fill a book. Better leave the grave alone than set up a monument to your own ignorance.

Of all places for jokes and fun, the queerest are tombstones, yet many a time gravestones have had such oddities carved upon them that one is led to think, the nearer the church, the further from common decency. This is a cruel verse, but I dare say a true one:

> "Here lies, return'd to clay,
> Miss Arabella Young,
> Who, on the first day of May
> Began to hold her tongue."

This is not much better:

> John Adams lies here, of the parish of Southwell,
> A *carrier* who *carried* his can to his mouth well;
> He *carried* so much, and he *carried* so fast,
> He could *carry* no more, so was *carried* at last;
> For the liquor he drunk being too much for one,
> He could not *carry* off, so he's now *carri-on*.

Why could not these people poke their fun somewhere else? A man's wit must be nearly dead when he can find no place for it but the grave. The body of the raggedest beggar is too sacred a thing to crack jokes upon. What a queer fish must Roger Martin have been, who lived iat Walworth, and put on his wife's tomb—

> "Here lies the wife of Roger Martin,
> She was a good wife to Roger—that's sartin,"

And whoever was the foolish creature at Ockham, one of the prettiest spots in these parts, who wrote these outrageous lines?

> "The Lord saw good, I was topping off wood,
> And down fell from the tree;
> I met with a check, and I broke my blessed neck,
> And so death topped off me."

There, that's enough, and quite as good as a feast. Here's proof positive that some fools are left alive to write on the monuments of those who are buried. Well may there be ghosts about. No wonder the sleepers get out of bed when they are so badly tucked in. I say let us have a law to let nobody put nonsense over the dead unless he likes to take out a certificate to be an ass, just like the licence to shoot partridges and pheasants. At the same time, let all puffery be saved for drapers' shops and quack doctors, and none be allowed at the grave. I say as our minister does—

> "Let no proud stone with sculptur'd virtues rise,
> To mark the spot wherein a sinner lies;
> Or if some boast must deck the sinner's grave,
> Boast of His love who died lost man to save."

One more Surrey rhyme, and John Ploughman leaves the churchyard to go about his work and turn up other sods. It is in St. Saviours, Southwark, and is, I think, a rare good one.

> "Like to the damask rose you see,
> Or like the blossom on the tree,
> Or like the dainty flow'r of May,
> Or like the morning of the day,
> Or like the sun, or like the shade,
> Or like the gourd which Jonah had;
> Even so is man, whose thread is spun,
> Drawn out, and cut, and so is done:
> The rose withers, the blossom blasteth,
> The flower fades, the morning hasteth,
> The sun sets, the shadow flies,
> The gourd consumes, and man he dies."

24
Very Ignorant People

I have heard tell of a man who did not know a great A from a bull's foot, and I know a good many who certainly could not tell what great A or little A either may mean; but some of these people are not the most ignorant in the world for all that. For instance, they know a cow's head from its tail, and one of the election gentlemen said lately that the candidate from London did not know that. They know that turnips don't grow on trees, and they can tell an overgrown radish from a beet root, and a rabbit from a hare, there are fine folk who play on pianos who hardly know as much as that. If they cannot read they can plough, and mow, and reap, and sow, and bring up seven children on ten shillings a week, and yet pay their way; and there's a sight of people who are much too ignorant to do that. Ignorance of spelling books is very bad, but ignorance of hard work is worse. Wisdom does not always speak Latin. People laugh at smock-frocks, and indeed they are about as ugly garments as could well be contrived, but some who wear them are not half such fools as people take them for. If no ignorant people ate bread but those who wear hobnail shoes, corn would be a fine deal cheaper. Wisdom in a poor man is like a diamond set in lead, only judges can see its value. Wisdom walks often in patched shoes, and men admire her not. But I say, never mind the coat, give me the man: nutshells are nothing, the kernel is everything. You need not go to Pirbright to find ignoramuses, there are heaps of them near St. Paul's.

I would have everybody able to read, write, and cipher; indeed, I don't think a man can know too much; but mark you the knowing of these things is not education; and there are millions of your reading and writing people who are as ignorant as neighbour Norton's calf, that did not know its own mother. This is as plain as the nose on your face, if you only think a little. To know how to read and write is like having tools to work with, but if you don't use these tools, and your eyes, and your ears too, you will be none the better off. Everybody should know what most concerns him and makes him most useful. If cats can catch mice find hens lay egged know the things which most suits what they were made for. It is little use for a horse to know how to fly it will do well enough if it can trot. A man on a farm ought to learn all that belongs to farming, a blacksmith should study a horse's foot, a dairyman should be well up on skimming the milk and making the butter, and a labourer's wife should be a good scholar in the sciences of boiling and baking, washing and mending; and John Ploughman ventures to say that those men and women who have not learned the duties of their callings are very ignorant people, even if they can tell the Greek name for a crocodile, or write an ode on a black beetle. It is too often very true—

"Jack has been to school
To learn to be a fool."

When a man falls into the water, to know how to swim
will be of more use to him than all his mathematics, and
yet how very few boys learn swimming! Girls are taught
dancing and French when stitching and English would be
a hundred per cent more use to them. When men have to
earn their livings, in these hard times, a good trade and
industrious habits will serve their turn a world better than
all the classics in Cambridge and Oxford; but who nowadays
advocates practical training at our schools? Schoolmasters
would go into fits if they were asked to teach poor people's
boys to hoe potatoes and plant cauliflowers, and yet
school boards would be doing a power of good if they did
something of the sort. If you want a dog to be a pointer
or a setter, you train him accordingly: why ever don't they
do the same with men? It ought to be, "Every man for his
business, and every man master of his business." Let Jack
and Tom learn geography by all means, but don't forget to
teach them how to black their own boots, and put a button
on their own trousers; and as for Jane and Sally, let them
sing and play the music if they like, but not till they can
darn a stocking and make a shirt. When they mend up that
Education Act, I hope they will put in a clause to teach
children practical common sense home duties as well as
the three R's. But there, what's the use of talking this
way, for if children are to learn common sense, where are
we to get the teachers? Very few people have any of it to
spare, and those who have are never likely to take to school
keeping. Lots of girls learn nothing except the folderols

which I think they call "accomplishments." There's poor Gent with six girls, and about fifty pounds a year to keep his family on, and yet not one of them can do a hand's turn, because their mother would go into fits lest Miss Sophia Elfrida should have chapped hands through washing the family linen, or lest Alexandra Theodora should spoil her complexion in picking a few gooseberries for a pudding. It's enough to make a cat laugh to hear the poor things talk about fashion and etiquette, when they are not half so well off as the higgler's daughters down the lane, who earn their own living, and are laying money by against the time when some young farmer will pick them up. Trust me, he who marries these hoity-toity young ladies will have as bad a bargain as if he married a wax doll. How the fat would be in the fire if Mrs. Gent heard me say it, but I do say it for all that, she and her girls are *ignorant, very ignorant,* because they do not know what would be of most service to them.

Every sprat nowadays calls itself a herring: every donkey thinks itself fit to be one of the Queen's horses; every candle reckons itself the sun. But when a man with his best coat on, and a paper collar, a glass in his eyes, a brass chain on his waistcoat, a cane in his hand, and emptiness in his head, fancies that people cannot see through his swaggers and brags, he must be *ignorant, very ignorant,* for he does not know himself. Dandies, dressed up to the top of the fashion, think themselves somebodies, but nobody else does. Dancing-masters and tailors may rig up a fop, but they cannot make a nothing into a man. You may colour a millstone as much as you like but you cannot improve it into a cheese.

When men believe in lawyers and money-lenders (whether Jews or Gentiles), and borrow money, and speculate, and think themselves lucky fellows, they are shamefully *ignorant*. The very gander on the common would not make such a stupid of himself, for he knows when anyone tries to pluck him, and won't lose his feathers and pride himself in the operation.

The man who spends his money with the publican, and thinks that the landlord's bows and "How do ye do, my good fellow?" mean true respect, is a perfect natural; for with them it is

> If you have money take a seat;
> If you have none take to your feet.

The fox admires the cheese; not the raven. The bait is not put into the trap to feed the mouse, but to catch him. We don't light a fire for the herring's comfort, but to roast him. Men do not keep pot-houses for the labourers' good; if they do, they certainly miss their aim. Why, then, should people drink "for the good of the house"? If I spend money for the good of house, let it be my own and not the landlord's. It's a bad well into which you must put water; and the beerhouse is a bad friend, because it takes your all, and leaves you nothing but heeltaps and headaches. He who calls those his friends who let him sit and drink by the hour, together is *ignorant, very ignorant*. Why, Red Lions, and Tigers, and Eagles, and Vultures, are all creatures of prey, and why do so many put themselves within the power of their jaws and talons?

He who believes that either Whigs or Tories will let us off with light taxes must have been born on the day after the last of March; and he who imagines that parish boards and vestries will ever have either heads or bowels must have been educated in an idiot asylum. He who believes in promises made at elections has long ears and may try to eat thistles. Mr. Plausible has been around asking all the working men for their votes and he will do all sorts of good things for them. Will he? Yes, the day after tomorrow — a little later than never. Poor men who expect the "friends of the working man" to do anything for them, must be *ignorant, very ignorant*. When they get their seats, of course they cannot stand up for their principles, except when it is to their own interest to do so.

To lend umbrellas and look to have them sent home, to do a man a good turn and expect another from him when you want it, to hope to stop some women's tongues, to try to please everybody, to hope to hear gossips speak well of you, or to get the truth of a story from common report, are all evidences of great ignorance.

Those who know the world best trust it least: those who trust it at all are not wise. As well trust a horse's heel or a dog's tooth. Trusting to others ruins many. He who leaves his business to bailiffs and servants and believes that it will be well done, must be *ignorant, very ignorant*. The mouse knows when the cat is out of the house, and servants know when the master is away. No sooner is the eye of the master gone than the hand of the workman slackens. I'll-go-myself, and "I'll-see-to-it," are two good servants on a farm. Those who lie in bed and reckon that their trade will carry on itself are *ignorant, very ignorant*.

Such as drink and live riotously, and wonder why their faces are so blotchy and their pockets so bare, would leave off wondering if they had two grains of wisdom. They might as well ask an elm-tree for pears as look to loose habits for health and wealth. Those who go to the public house for happiness climb a tree to find fish. We might put all their wit in an egg-shell, or they would never be such dupes as to hunt after comfort where it is no more to be found than a cow in a crow's nest; but, alas! good-for-nothings are common as mice in a hay stack. I only wish we could pack them off to Lubber-land, where they have half-a-crown a day for sleeping. If someone could let them see the sure result of ill-living, perhaps they might reform; and yet I don't know, for they do see it, and yet go on all the same; like a moth that gets singed and flies into the candle again. Certainly for loitering lushes to expect to thrive by keeping their hands in their pockets, or their noses in pewter pots proves them to be *ignorant, very ignorant.*

When I see a young lady with a flower garden on her roof, and a draper's shop on her body, tossing her head about as if she thought everybody was charmed with her, I am sure she must be *ignorant, very ignorant.* Sensible men don't marry a wardrobe or a bonnet-box; they want a woman of sense, and these dress sensibly.

To my mind, those who sneer at religion, and set themselves up to be too knowing to believe in the Bible are shallow fellows. They generally use big words, and bluster a great deal, but if they fancy they can overturn the faith of thinking people, who have tried and proved the power of the grace of God, they must be *ignorant, very ignorant.* He who looks at the sunrise and the sunset, and does not see the footprints of God, must be inwardly more blind than a mole, and only fit to live underground.

God seems to talk to me in every primrose and daisy, to smile upon me from every star, to whisper to me in every breath of morning air and call aloud to me in every storm. It is strange that. so many educated gentlemen see God nowhere, while John the ploughman feels Him everywhere. John has no wish to change places, for the sense of God's presence is his comfort and joy. They say that man is the god of the dog: that man must be worse than a dog who will not listen to the voice of God, for a dog follows at his master's whistle. They call themselves philosophers, don't they? Their proper name is fools, for the fool hath said in his heart, "There is no God."

The sheep know when rain is coming, the swallows foresee the winter, and even the pigs, they say, can see the wind; how much worse than a brute must he be who lives where God is everywhere present and yet sees Him not!

So you see a man may be; a great hand at learning, and yet be *ignorant, very ignorant*.

John Ploughman's Pictures;

or

More of his Plain Talk for Plain People

by
C. H. Spurgeon

Preface

"John Ploughman's Talk" has not only obtained an immense circulation, but it has exercised an influence for good. Although its tone is rather moral than religious, it has led many to take the first steps by which men climb to better things, and this fact has moved me to attempt a second book of the same character. I have continued to use the simplest form of our mother tongue, so that if any readers must need have refined language they had better leave these pages before they are quite disgusted. To smite evil — and especially the monster evil of drink — has been my earnest endeavour, and assuredly there is need. It may be that the vice of drunkenness is not more common than it used to be; but it is sufficiently rampant to cause sorrow in every Christian bosom, and to lead all lovers of their race to lift up their voices against it. I hope that the plain speech of JOHN PLOUGHMAN will help in that direction.

It is quite out of the question for the compiler of such proverbial talk as this to acknowledge the sources from which the quaint sayings have been derived, for they are too numerous. I have gathered expressions and verses here, there, and everywhere and perhaps the most simple way is to deny all claim to originality, and confess myself a gatherer of other men's stuffs. It is not quite so, but that is near enough. I have, however, borrowed many rhymes from "Thomas Tusser's Points of Good Husbandry," a book which is out of date, and forgotten, and never likely to be reprinted.

I have somewhat indulged the mirthful vein, but ever with so serious a purpose that I ask no forgiveness. Those who see a virtue in dullness have full permission to condemn, for a sufficient number will approve.

May the kindness shown to the former volume be extended to this also.

C, H. SPURGEON.

1
If the cap fits, wear it.

Friendly Readers,
 Last time I made a book I trod on some people's
corns and bunions, and they wrote me angry letters,

asking, "Did you mean me?" This time, to save them the expense of a halfpenny card, I will begin my book by saying —

> Whether I please or whether I tease,
> I'll give you my honest mind;
> If the cap should fit, pray wear it a bit,
> If not, you can leave it behind.

No offence is meant; but if anything in these pages should come home to a man, let him not send it next door, but get a coop for his own chickens. What is the use of reading or hearing for other people? We do not eat and drink for them: why should we lend them our ears and not our mouths? Please then, good friend, if you find a hoe on these premises, weed your own garden with it.

I was speaking with Will Shepherd the other day about our master's old donkey, and I said, "He is so old and stubborn, he really is not worth his keep." "No," said Will, "and worse still, he is so vicious, that I feel sure he'll do somebody a mischief one of these days." You know they say that walls have ears; we were talking rather loud, but we did not know that there were ears to haystacks. We stared, I tell you, when we saw Joe Scroggs come from behind the stack, looking as red as a turkey-cock, and raving like mad. He burst out swearing at Will and me, like a cat spitting at a dog. His monkey was up and no mistake. He'd let us know that he was as good a man as either of us, or the two put together, for the matter of that. Talking about *him* in that way; he'd do — I don't know what. I told old Joe we had never thought of him, nor said a word about him, and he might just as well save his breath to cool his porridge, for nobody meant him any harm. This only made him call me a liar, and roar the louder. My friend, Will, was walking away, holding his sides, but when he saw that Scroggs was still in a fume, he laughed outright, and turned round on him and said, "Why, Joe, we were talking about master's old donkey, and not about you; but, upon my word, I shall never see that donkey again without thinking of Joe Scroggs." Joe puffed and blowed, but perhaps he thought it an awkward job, for he backed out of it, and Will and I went off to our work in rather a merry cue, for old Joe had blundered on the truth about himself for once in his life.

The aforesaid Will Shepherd has sometimes come down rather heavy upon me in his remarks, but it has done me good. It is partly through his home thrusts that I have come to write this new book, for he thought I was idle; perhaps I am, and perhaps I am not. Will forgets that I have other fish to fry and tails to butter; and he does not recollect that a ploughman's mind wants to lie fallow a little, and can't give a crop every year. It is hard to make rope when your hemp is all used up, or pancakes without batter, or rook pie without the birds; and so I found it hard to write more when I had said just about all I knew. Giving much to the poor doth increase a man's store, but it is not the same with writing; at least, I am such a poor scribe that I don't find it come because I pull. If your thoughts only flow by drops, you can't pour them out in bucketfuls.

However, Will has ferreted me out, and I am obliged to him so far. I told him the other day, what the winkle said to the pin: "Thank you for drawing me out, but you are rather sharp about it." Still, Master Will is not far from the mark: after three hundred thousand people had bought my book it certainly was time to write another: so, though I am not a hatter, I will again turn cap-maker, and those who have heads may try on my wares: those who have none won't touch them.

So, friends,
I am,
Yours, rough and ready,

JOHN PLOUGHMAN.

2

Burn a candle at both ends,
and it will soon be gone.

Well may he scratch his head who burns his candle at both ends; but, do what he may, his light will soon be gone, and he will be all in the dark. Young Jack Careless squandered his property, and now he is without a shoe to his foot. His was a case of "easy come, easy go: soon gotten, soon spent." He that earns an estate will keep it better than he that inherits it. As the Scotchman says, "He that gets gear before he gets wit is but a short time master of it," and so it was with Jack. His money burnt holes in his pocket. He could not get rid of it fast enough himself, and so he got a pretty set to help him, which they did by helping themselves. His fortune went like a pound of meat in a kennel of hounds. He was everybody's friend, and now he is everybody's fool.

He came in to old Alderman Greedy's money, for he was his nephew; but, as the old saying is, the fork followed the rake, the spender was heir to the hoarder. God has been very merciful to some of us in never letting money come rolling in upon us, for most men are carried off their legs if they meet with a great wave of fortune. Many of us would have been bigger sinners if we had been trusted with larger purses. Poor Jack had plenty of pence, but little sense. Money is easier made than made use of. What is hard to gather is easy to scatter. The old gentleman had lined his nest well, but Jack made the feathers fly like flakes of snow in winter-time. He got rid of his money by shovelfuls and then by cartloads. After spending the interest, he began swallowing the capital, and so killed the goose that laid the golden eggs. He squandered his silver and gold, in ways which must never be told. It would not go fast enough, and so he bought race-horses to run away with it. He got into the hands of blacklegs, and fell into company of which we shall say but little; only when such madams smile, men's purses weep: these are a well without a bottom, and the more a fool throws in, the more he may. The greatest beauty often causes the greatest ruin. Play, women, and wine are enough to make a prince a pauper.

Always taking out and never putting back soon empties the biggest sack, and so Jack found it; but he took no notice till his last shilling bade him good-bye, and then he said he had been robbed; like silly Tom who put his finger in the fire and said it was his bad luck.

> His money once flashed like dew in the sun;
> When bills became due, of cash he had none.

"Drink and let drink" was his motto; every day was a holiday and every holiday a feast. The best of wines and dearest of dainties suited his tooth, for he meant to lead a pig's life, which they say is short and sweet. Truly, he went the whole hog. The old saying is, "a glutton young, a beggar old," and he seemed set upon proving it true. A fat kitchen makes a lean will; but he can make his will on his finger-nail, and leave room for a dozen codicils. In fact, he will never want a will at all, for he will leave nothing behind him but old scores. Of all his estate there is not enough left to bury him with. What he threw away in his prosperity would have kept a coat on his back and a dumpling in his pot to his life's end; but he never looked beyond his nose, and could not see to the end of that. He laughed at prudence, and now prudence frowns at him. Punishment is lame but it comes at last. He pays the cost of his folly in body and in soul, in purse and in person, and yet he is still a fool, and would dance to the same tune again if he had another chance. His light purse brings him a heavy heart, but he couldn't have his cake and eat it too. As he that is drunk at night is dry in the morning, so he that lavished money when he had it feels the want of it all the more when it is gone. His old friends have quite dropped him; they have squeezed the orange, and now they throw away the peel. As well look for milk from a pigeon as help from a fellow who loved you for your beer. Pot friends will let you go to pot, and kick you when you are down.

Jack has worse wants than the want of money, for his character is gone, and he is like a rotten nut, not worth the cracking: the neighbours say he is a ne'er-do-well, not worth calling out of a cabbage garden. Nobody will employ him, for he would not earn his salt, and so he goes from pillar to post, and has not a place to lay his head in. A good name is better than a girdle of gold, and when that is gone, what has a man left?

What has he left? Nothing upon earth! Yet the prodigal son has still a Father in heaven. Let him arise and go to him, ragged as he is. He may smell of the swine-trough, and yet he may run straight home, and he shall not find the door locked. The great Father will joyfully meet him, and kiss him, and cleanse him, and clothe him, and give him to begin a new and better life. When a sinner is at his worst he is not too bad for the Saviour, if he will but turn from his wickedness and cry unto God for mercy. It's a long lane that has no turning, but the best of all turns is to turn unto the Lord with all your heart. This the great Father will help the penitent prodigal to do. If the candle has been burned all away, the Sun in the heavens is still alight. Look, poor profligate: look to Jesus, and live. His salvation is without money and without price.

Though you may not have a penny to bless yourself with, the Lord Jesus will bless you freely. The depths of your misery are not so deep as the depth of God's mercy. If you are faithful and just in confessing the sins you would have forgiven, God will be faithful and just in forgiving the sins which you confess.

But, pray, do not go on another day as you are, for this very day may be your last. If you will not heed a plain word from John Ploughman, which he means for your good, yet recollect this old-fashioned rhyme, which was copied from a grave-stone:

> The loss of gold is great,
> The loss of health is more,
> But the loss of Christ is such a loss
> As no man can restore.

3

Hunchback sees not his own hump,
but he sees his neighbour's.

He points at the man in front of him, but he is a good deal more of a guy himself. He should not laugh at the crooked until he is straight himself, and not then. I hate to hear a raven croak at a crow for being black.

A blind man should not blame his brother for squinting, and he who has lost his legs should not sneer at the lame. Yet so it is, the rottenest bough cracks first, and he who should be the last to speak is the first to rail. Bespattered hogs bespatter others, and he who is full of fault finds fault. They are most apt to speak ill of others who do most ill themselves.

> "We're very keen our neighbour's hump to see,
> We're blind to that upon our back alone;
> E'en though the lump far greater be,
> It still remains to us unknown."

It does us much hurt to judge our neighbours, because it flatters our conceit, and our pride grows quite fast enough without feeding. We accuse others to excuse ourselves. We are such fools as to dream that we are better because others are worse, and we talk as if we could get up by pulling others down. What is the good of spying holes in people's coats when we can't mend them? Talk of my debts if you mean to pay them; if not, keep your red rag behind your ivory ridge. A friend's faults should not be advertised, and even a stranger's should not be published. He who brays at an ass is an ass himself, and he who makes a fool of another is a fool himself. Don't get into the habit of laughing at people, for the old saying is, "Hanging's stretching and mocking's catching."

> Some must have their joke whoever they poke;
> For the sake of fun mischief is done,
> And to air their wit full many they hit.

Jesting is too apt to turn into jeering, and what was meant to tickle makes a wound. It is a pity when my

mirth is another man's misery. Before a man cracks a joke
he should consider how he would like it himself, for many
who give rough blows have very thin skins. Give only
what you would be willing to take: some men throw salt
on others, but they smart if a pinch of it falls on their
own raw places. When they get a Roland for their Oliver,
or a tit for their tat, they don't like it; yet nothing is more
just. Biters deserve to be bitten.

We may chide a friend, and so prove our friendship,
but it must be done very daintily, or we may lose our
friend for our pains. Before we rebuke another we must
consider, and take heed that we are not guilty of the same
thing, for he who cleanses a blot with inky fingers makes
it worse. To despise others is a worse fault than any we
are likely to see in them, and to make merry over their
weaknesses shows our own weakness and our own malice
too. Wit should be a shield for defence, and not a sword
for offence. A mocking word cuts worse than a scythe,
and the wound is harder to heal. A blow is much sooner
forgotten than a jeer. Mocking is shocking. Our minister
says "to laugh at infirmity or deformity is an enormity."
He is a man who ought to know a thing or two, and he
puts a matter as pat as butter.

> "Who ridicules his neighbour's frailty
> Scoffs at his own in more or less degree:
> Much wiser he who others' lets alone,
> And tries his hardest to correct his own."

4

It is hard for an empty sack
to stand upright.

Sam may try a fine while before he will make one of his empty sacks stand upright. If he were not half daft he would have left off that job before he began it, and not have been an Irishman either. He will come to his wit's end before he sets the sack on its end. The old proverb, printed at the top, was made by a man who had burnt his fingers with debtors, and it just means that when folks have no money and are over head and ears in debt, as often as not they leave off being upright, and tumble over one way or another. He that has but four and spends five will soon need no purse, but he will most likely begin to use his wits to keep himself afloat, and take to all sorts of dodges to manage it.

Nine times out of ten they begin by making promises to pay on a certain day when it is certain they have nothing to pay with. They are as bold at fixing the time as if they had my lord's income: the day comes round as sure as Christmas, and then they haven't a penny-piece in the world, and so they make all sorts of excuses and begin to promise again. Those who are quick to promise are generally slow to perform. They promise mountains and perform mole-hills. He who gives you fair words and nothing more feeds you with an empty spoon, and hungry creditors soon grow tired of that game. Promises don't fill the belly. Promising men are not great favourites if they are not performing men. When such a fellow is called a liar he thinks he is hardly done by; and yet he is so, as sure as eggs are eggs, and there's no denying it, as the boy said when the gardener caught him up the cherry-tree. People don't think much of a man's piety when his promises are like pie-crust, made to be broken: they generally turn crusty themselves and give him a bit of their mind. Like old Tusser, who said of such an one:

> "His promise to trust to is slippery as ice,
> His credit much like to the chance of the dice."

Creditors have better memories than debtors, and when they have been taken in more than once they think it is time that the fox went to the furrier, and they had their share of his skin. Waiting for your money does not sweeten a man's temper, and a few lies on the top of it turn the milk of human kindness into sour stuff. Here is an old-fashioned saying which a bad payer may put in his pipe, and smoke or not, as he likes:

> "He that promiseth till no man will trust him,
> He that lieth till no man will believe him,
> He that borroweth till no man will lend him,
> Let him go where no man knoweth him."

Hungry dogs will eat dirty puddings, and people who are hard up very often do dirty actions. Blessed be God, there is some cloth still made which will not shrink in the wetting, and some honesty which holds on under misfortune; but too often debt is the worst kind of poverty, because it breeds deceit. Men do not like to face their circumstances, and so they turn their backs on the truth. They try all sorts of schemes to get out of their difficulties and like the Banbury tinker, they make three holes in the saucepan to mend one. They are like Pedley, who burnt a penny candle in looking for a farthing. They borrow of Peter to pay Paul, and then Peter is let in for it. To avoid a brook they leap into a river, for they borrow at ruinous interest to pay off those who squeeze them tight. By ordering goods which they cannot pay for, and selling them for whatever they can get, they may put off one evil day, but they only bring on another. One trick needs another trick to back it up, and thus they go on over shoes and then over boots. Hoping that something will turn up, they go on raking for the moon in a ditch, and all the luck that comes to them is like Johnny Toy's, who lost a shilling and found a two-penny loaf. Any short cut tempts them out of the high road of honesty, and they find after a while that they have gone miles out of their way. At last people fight shy of them, and say that they are as honest as a cat when the meat is out of reach, and they murmur that plain dealing is dead, and died without issue. Who wonders? People who are bitten once are in no hurry to put their fingers into the same mouth again. You don't trust a horse's heel after it has kicked you, nor lean on a staff which has once broken. Too much cunning overdoes its work, and in the long run there is no craft which is so wise as simple honesty.

I would not be hard on a poor fellow, nor pour water on a drowned mouse; if through misfortune the man can't pay, why he can't pay, and let him say so, and do the honest thing with what little he has, and kind hearts will feel for him. A wise man does at first what a fool does at last. The worst of it is, that debtors will hold on long after it is honest to do so, and they try to persuade themselves that their ship will come home, or their cats will grow into cows. It is hard to sail over the sea in an eggshell, and it is not much easier to pay your way when your capital is all gone. Out of nothing comes nothing, and you may turn your nothing over a long time before it will grow into a ten-pound note. The way to Babylon will never bring you to Jerusalem, and borrowing, and diving deeper into debt, will never get a man out of difficulties.

The world is a ladder for some to go up and some to go down, but there is no need to lose your character because you lose your money. Some people jump out of the frying-pan into the fire; for fear of being paupers they become rogues. You find them slippery customers; you can't bind them to anything: you think you have got them, but you can't hold them any longer than you can keep a cat in a wheelbarrow. They can jump over nine hedges, and nine more after that. They always deceive you, and then plead the badness of the times, or the sickness of their family. You cannot help them, for there's no telling where they are. It is always best to let them come to the end of their tether, for when they are cleaned out of their old rubbish they may perhaps begin in a better fashion. You cannot get out of a sack what is not in it, and when a man's purse is as bare as the back of your hand, the longer you patch him up the barer he will become, like Bill Bones, who cut up his coat to patch his waistcoat, and then used his trousers to mend his coat, and at last had to lie in bed for want of a rag to cover him.

Let the poor, unfortunate tradesman hold to his honesty as he would to his life. The straight road is the shortest cut. Better break stones on the road than break the law of God. Faith in God should save a Christian man from anything like a dirty action; let him not even think of playing a trick, for you cannot touch pitch without being defiled therewith. Christ and a crust is riches, but a broken character is the worst of bankruptcy. All is not lost while uprightness remains; but still *it is hard to make an empty sack stand upright*.

There are other ways of using the old saying. It is hard for a hypocrite to keep up his profession. Empty sacks can't stand upright in a church any better than in a granary. Prating does not make saints, or there would be plenty of them. Some talkatives have not religion enough to flavour soup for a sick grasshopper, and they have to be mighty cunning to keep the game going. Long prayers and loud professions only deceive the simple, and those who see further than the surface soon spy out the wolf under the sheepskin.

All hope of salvation by our own good works is a foolish attempt to make an empty sack stand upright. We are undeserving, ill-deserving, hell-deserving sinners at best. The law of God must be kept without a single failure if we hope to be accepted by it; but there is not one among us who has lived a day without sin. No, we are a lot of empty sacks, and unless the merits of Christ are put into us to fill us up, we cannot stand in the sight of God. The law condemns us already, and to hope for salvation by it is to run to the gallows to prolong our lives. There is a full Christ for empty sinners, but those who hope to fill themselves will find their hopes fail them.

5

He who would please all, will lose his donkey
and be laughed at for his pains.

Here's a queer picture, and this is the story which
goes with it; you shall have it just as I found it in
an old book. "An old man and his young son were driving
an ass before them to the next market to sell. 'Why have

you no more wit,' says one to the man upon the way, 'than you and your son to trudge it a-foot, and let the ass go light?' So the old man set his son upon the ass, and footed it himself. 'Why, sirrah,' says another after this, to the boy, 'ye lazy rogue, you, must you ride, and let your old father go a-foot?' The old man upon this took down his son, and got up himself. 'Do you see,' says a third, 'how the lazy old knave rides himself, and the poor young fellow has much ado to creep after him?' The father, upon this, took up his son behind him. The next they met asked the old man whether the ass were his own or no. He said, 'Yes.' 'Troth, there's little sign on't,' says the other, 'by your loading him thus.' 'Well,' says the old man to himself, 'and what am I to do now? for I'm laughed at, if either the ass be empty, or if *one* of us rides, or *both*;' and so he came to the conclusion to bind the ass's legs together with a cord, and they tried to carry him to market with a pole upon their shoulders, betwixt them. This was sport to everybody that saw it, inasmuch that the old man in great wrath threw down the ass into a river, and so went his way home again. The good man, in fine, was willing to please everybody, but had the ill fortune to please nobody, and lost his ass into the bargain."

He who will not go to bed till he pleases everybody will have to sit up a great many nights. Many men, many minds; many women, many whims; and so if we please one we are sure to set another grumbling. We had better wait till they are all of one mind before we mind them, or we shall be like the man who hunted many hares at once and caught none. Besides, the fancies of men alter, and folly is never long pleased with the same thing, but

changes its palate, and grows sick of what it doted on.
Will Shepherd says he once tried to serve two masters,
but, says he, "I soon had enough of it, and I declared that,
if I was pardoned this once, the next time they caught me
at it they might pickle me in salt and souse me in boiling
vinegar."

> "He who would general favour win
> And not himself offend,
> Today the task he may begin,
> He'll never, never end."

If we dance to every fiddle we shall soon be lame in both
legs. Good nature may be a great misfortune if we do not
mix prudence with it.

> He that all men would please
> Shall never find ease.

It is right to be obliging, but we are not obliged to be
every man's lackey. Put your hand quickly to your hat, for
that is courtesy; but don't bow your head at every man's
bidding, for that is slavery. He who hopes to please all
should first fit the moon with a suit of clothes, or fill
a bottomless barrel with buckets with their hoops off. To
live upon the praises of others is to feed on the air; for
what is praise but the breath of men's nostrils? That's
poor stuff to make a dinner of. To set traps for claps, and
to faint if you don't get them, is a childish thing; and to
change your coat to please new company is as mean as
dirt. Change for the better as often as you like, but mind
it is better before you change. Tom of Bedlam never did
a madder thing than he who tried to please a thousand
masters at once: one is quite enough. If a man pleases

God he may let the world wag its own way, and frown or flatter, as the maggot bites. What is there, after all, to frighten a man in a fool's grin, or in the frown of a poor mortal like yourself? If it mattered at all what the world says of us, it would be some comfort that when a good man is buried people say, "He was not a bad fellow after all." When the cow is dead we hear how much milk she gave. When the man's gone to heaven folks know their loss, and wonder how it was they did not treat him better.

The way of pleasing men is hard, but blessed are they who please God. He is not a free man who is afraid to think for himself, for if his thoughts are in bonds the man is not free. A man of God is a manly man. A true man does what he thinks to be right, whether the pigs grunt or the dogs howl. Are you afraid to follow out your conscience because Tom, Jack, and Harry, or Mary, Ann and Betsy, would laugh at you? Then you are not the seventy-fifth cousin to John Ploughman, who goes on his way whistling merrily, though many find fault with himself, and his plough, and his horses, and his harness, and his boots, and his coat, and his waistcoat, and his hat, and his head, and every hair on it. John says it amuses them and doesn't hurt him; but depend on it you will never catch John or his boys carrying the donkey.

6

All are not hunters that blow the horn.

He does not look much like a hunter! Nimrod would never own him. But how he blows! Goodness, gracious, what a row! as the linnet said when he heard a donkey singing his evening hymn. There's more goes to ploughing than knowing how to whistle, and hunting is not all tally-ho and horn-blowing. Appearances are deceitful. Outward show is not everything. All are not butchers that carry a steel, and all are not bishops that wear aprons. You must not buy goods by the label; for I have heard that the finer the trade-mark the worse the article. Never have we seen more horn or less hunter than in our picture. Blow away, my hearty, till your toes look out of your boots; there's no fear of your killing either fox or stag!

Now, the more people blow, the more they may, but he is a fool who believes all they say. As a rule, the smallest boy carries the biggest fiddle, and he who makes most boast has least roast. He who has least wisdom has most vanity. John Lackland is wonderfully fond of being called Esquire, and there's none so pleased at being dubbed a doctor as the man who least deserves it. Many a D.D. is fiddle-dee-dee. I have heard say, "Always talk big and somebody will think you great," but my old friend Will Shepherd says, "Save your wind for running up a hill, and don't give us big words off a weak stomach. Look," said he once to me, "There's Solomon Braggs holding up his head like a hen drinking water, but there's nothing in it. With him it's much din and little done."

> "Of all speculations the market holds forth,
> The best that I know for a lover of pelf,
> Were to buy up this Braggs at the price he is worth,
> And sell him — at that which he sets on himself."

Before honour is humility, but a prating fool shall fall, and when he falls very few will be in a hurry to pick him up.

A long tongue generally goes with a short hand. We are most of us better at saying than doing. We can all tattle away from the battle, but many fly when the fight is nigh. Some are all sound and fury, and when they have bragged their brag all is over, and *amen*. The fat Dutchman was the wisest pilot in Flushing, only he never went to sea; and the Irishman was the finest rider in Connaught, only he would never trust himself on a horse, because, as he said, "he generally fell off before he got on." A bachelor's wife is always well managed, and old maids always bring up their children in prime style. We think we can do what we are not called to, and if by chance the thing falls to our lot we do worse than those we blamed. Hence it's wise to be slow in foretelling what we will do, for —

> "Thus saith the proverb of the wise,
> 'Who boasteth least tells fewest lies.'"

There is another old rhyme which is as full of reason as a pod is full of peas, -

> "Little money is soonest spended;
> Fewest words are soonest mended."

Of course, every potter praises his own pot, and we can all toot a little on our own trumpet, but some blow as if nobody ever had a horn but themselves. "After me the flood," says the mighty big man, and whether it be so or no we have floods enough while he lives. I mean floods of words, words, words, enough to drown all your senses. O that the man had a mouth big enough to say all he has to say at one go, and have done with it; but then one had need get to the other end of the world till his talk had run itself dry. O for a quiet hay-loft, or a saw-pit, or a dungeon, where the sound of the jawbone would no more be heard. They say a brain is worth little if you have not a tongue; but what is a tongue worth without a brain? Bellowing is all very well, but the cow for me is that which fills the pail. A braying ass eats little hay, and that's a saving in fodder; but a barking dog catches no game, and that's a loss to the owner. Noise is no profit, and talk hinders work.

When a man's song is in his praise, let the hymn be short metre, and let the tune be in the minor key. He who talks for ever about himself has a foolish subject, and is likely to worry and weary all around him. Good wine needs no bush, and a man who can do well seldom boasts about it. The emptiest tub makes the loudest noise. Those who give themselves out to be fine shots kill very few birds, and many a crack ploughman does a shorter day's work than plain John, though he is nothing off the common; and so on the whole it is pretty clear that the best huntsmen are not those who are for everlastingly blowing the horn.

7

A handsaw is a good thing,
but not to shave with.

O ur friend will cut more than he will eat, and shave off something more than hair, and then he will blame the saw. His brains don't lie in his beard, nor yet in the skull above it, or he would see that his saw will only make sores. There's sense in choosing your tools, for a pig's tail will never make a good arrow, nor will his ear make a silk purse. You can't catch rabbits with drums, nor pigeons with plums. A good thing is not good out of its place. It is much the same with lads and girls; you can't put all boys to one trade, nor send all girls to the same service. One chap will make a London clerk, and another will do better to plough, and sow, and reap, and mow, and be a farmer's boy. It's no use forcing them; a snail will never run a race, nor a mouse drive a wagon.

> "Send a boy to the well against his will,
> The pitcher will break and the water spill."

With unwilling hounds it is hard to hunt hares. To go against nature and inclination is to row against wind and tide. They say you may praise a fool till you make him useful: I don't know so much about that, but I do know that if I get a bad knife I generally cut my finger, and a blunt axe is more trouble than profit. No, let me shave with a razor if I shave at all, and do my work with the best tools I can get.

Never set a man to work he is not fit for, for he will never do it well. They say that if pigs fly they always go with their tails forward, and awkward workmen are much the same. Nobody expects cows to catch crows, or hens to wear hats. There's reason in roasting eggs, and there should be reason in choosing servants. Don't put a round peg into a square hole, nor wind up your watch with a cork-screw, nor set a tender-hearted man to whip wife-beaters, nor a bear to be a relieving-officer, nor a publican to judge of the licensing laws. Get the right man in the right place, and then all goes as smooth as skates on ice; but the wrong man puts all awry, as the sow did when she folded the linen.

It is a temptation to many to trust them with money: don't put them to take care of it if you ever wish to see it again. Never set a cat to watch cream, nor a pig to gather peaches, for if the cream and the peaches go a-missing you will have yourself to thank for it. It is a sin to put people where they are likely to sin. If you believe the old saying, that when you set a beggar on horseback he will ride to the devil, don't let him have a horse of yours.

If you want a thing well done do it yourself, and pick your tools. It is true that a man must row with such oars as he has, but he should not use the boat-hook for a paddle. Take not the tongs to poke the fire, nor the poker to put on the coals. A newspaper on Sunday is as much out of place as a warming-pan on the first of August, or a fan on a snowy day: the Bible suits the Sabbath a deal better.

He who tries to make money by betting uses a wrong tool, and is sure to cut his fingers. As well hope to grow golden pippins on the bottom of the sea as to make gain among gamblers if you are an honest man. Hard work and thrifty habits are the right razor, gambling is a handsaw.

Some things want doing gently, and telling a man of his faults is one of them. You would not fetch a hatchet to break open an egg, nor kill a fly on your boy's forehead with a sledge-hammer, and so you must not try to mend your neighbour's little fault by blowing him up sky-high. Never fire off a musket to kill a midge, and don't raise a hue and cry about the half of nothing.

Do not throw away a saw because it is not a razor, for it will serve your turn another day, and cut your ham-bone if it won't shave off your stubble. A whetstone, though it cannot cut, may sharpen a knife that will. A match gives little light itself, but it may light a candle to brighten up the room. Use each thing and each man according to common sense and you will be uncommonly sensible. You don't milk horses nor ride cows, and by the same rule you must make of every man what he is meant for, and the farm will be as right as a trivet.

Everything has its use, but no one thing is good for all purposes. The baby said, "The cat crew and the cock rocked the cradle," but old folks knew better: the cat is best at mousing and the cock at rousing. That's for that, as salt is for herrings, and sugar for gooseberries, and Nan for Nicholas. Don't choose your tools by their looks, for that's best which does best. A silver trowel lays very few bricks. You cannot curry a horse with a tortoise-shell comb, or fell oaks with a pen-knife, or open oysters with a gold tooth-pick. *Fine* is not so good as *fit* when work is to be done. A good workman will get on pretty well with a poor tool, and a brave soldier never lacks a weapon: still, the best is good enough for me, and John Ploughman does not care to use a clumsy tool because it looks pretty. Better ride on an ass that carries you than on a steed which throws you; it is far better to work with an old-fashioned spade which suits your hand than with a new-fangled invention you don't understand.

In trying to do good to your fellow-men the gospel is out of sight the best instrument to work with. The new doctrine which they call "modern thought" is nothing better than a handsaw, and it won't work a bit. This fine new nothing of a gospel would not save a mouse, nor move the soul of a tom-tit; but the glorious gospel of Jesus Christ is suited to man's need, and by God's grace does its work famously. Let every preacher and teacher keep to it, for they will never find a better. Try to win men with its loving words and precious promises, and there's no fear of labour in vain. Some praise the balm of Gilead, or man's morality; many try the Roman salve, or the oil of Babylon; and others use a cunning ointment mixed by learned philosophers; but for his own soul's wounds, and for the hurts of others, John Ploughman knows but one cure, and that is given gratis by the good Physician to all who ask for it. A humble faith in Christ Jesus will soon bring you this sovereign remedy. Use no other, for no other is of use.

8
Don't cut off your nose
to spite your face.

Anger is a short madness. The less we do when we go mad the better for everybody, and the less we go mad the better for ourselves. He is far gone who hurts himself to wreak his vengeance on others. The old saying is "Don't cut off your head because it aches," and another says "Set not your house on fire to spite the moon." If things go awry, it is a poor way of mending to make them worse, as the man did who took to drinking because he could not marry the girl he liked. He must be a fool who cuts off his nose to spite his face, and yet this is what Dick did when he had vexed his old master, and because he was chid must needs give up his place, throw himself out of work, and starve his wife and family. Jane had been idle, and she knew it, but sooner than let her mistress speak to her, she gave warning, and lost as good a service as a maid could wish for. Old Griggs was wrong, and could not deny it, and yet because the parson's sermon fitted him rather close, he took the sulks and vowed he would never hear the good man again. It was his own loss, but he wouldn't listen to reason, but was as wilful as a pig.

Do nothing when you are out of temper, and then you will have the less to undo. Let a hasty man's passion be a warning to you; if he scalds you, take heed that you do not let your own pot boil over. Many a man has given himself a box on the ear in his blind rage, ay, and ended his own life out of spite. He who cannot curb his temper carries gun-powder in his bosom, and he is neither safe for himself nor his neighbours. When passion comes in at the door, what little sense there is indoors flies out at the window. By-and-by a hasty man cools and comes to himself, like MacGibbon's gruel when he put it out of the window, but if his nose is off in the meantime, who is to put it on again? He will only be sorry once and that will be all the rest of his life. Anger does a man more hurt than that which made him angry. It opens his mouth and shuts his eyes, and fires his heart, and drowns his sense, and makes his wisdom folly. Old Tompkins told me that he was sorry that he lost his temper, and I could not help thinking that the pity was that he ever found it again, for it was like an old shoe with the sole gone and the upper leathers worn out, only fit for a dunghill. A hot-tempered man would be all the better for a new heart, and a right spirit. Anger is a fire which cooks no victuals, and comforts no household: it cuts and curses and kills, and no one knows what it may lead to; therefore, good reader, don't let it lodge in your bosom, and if it ever comes there, pass the vagrant on to the next parish.

> Gently, gently, little pot,
> Why so hasty to be hot?
> Over you will surely boil,
> And I know not what you'll spoil.

The old gent in our picture has a fine nose of his own, and though he will be a fool to cut it off, he would be wise to cut off the supplies which have made it such a size. That glass and jug on the table are the paint-pots that he colours his nose with, and everybody knows, whether he knows it or knows it not, that his nose is the outward and visible sign of a good deal of inward and spirituous drink, and the sooner he drops his drops the better. So here we will cut off, not our nose, but the present subject.

9

He has a hole under his nose
and his money runs into it

This is the man who is always dry, because he takes so much heavy wet. He is a loose fellow who is fond of getting tight. He is no sooner up than his nose is in the cup, and his money begins to run down the hole which is just under his nose. He is not a blacksmith, but he has a spark in his throat, and all the publican's barrels can't put it out. If a pot of beer is a yard of land, he must have swallowed more acres than a ploughman could get over for many a day, and still he goes on swallowing until he takes to wallowing. All goes down Gutter Lane. Like the snipe, he lives by suction. If you ask him how he is, he says he would be quite right if he could moisten his mouth. His purse is a bottle, his bank is the publican's till, and his casket is a cask: pewter is his precious metal, and his pearl* is a mixture of gin and beer. The dew of his youth comes from Ben Nevis, and the comfort of his soul is cordial gin. He is a walking barrel, a living drain-pipe, a moving swill-tub. They say "loth to drink and loth to leave off," but he never needs persuading to begin, and as to ending — that is out of the question while he can borrow two-pence. This is the gentleman who sings —

> He that buys land buys many stones,
> He that buys meat buys many bones,
> He that buys eggs buys many shells,
> He that buys good ale buys nothing else.

He will never be hanged for leaving his drink behind him. He drinks in season and out of season: in summer because he is hot, and in winter because he is cold. A drop of beer never comes too soon, and he would get up in the middle of the night for more, only he goes to bed too tipsy. He has heard that if you get wet-footed a glass of whisky in your boots will keep you from catching cold, and he argues that the best way to get one glass of the spirit into

---

* purl

each boot is to put two doses where it will run into your legs. He is never long without an excuse for another pot, or if perchance he does not make one, another lushington helps him.

> Some drink when friends step in,
> And some when they step out;
> Some drink because they're thin,
> And some because they're stout.
>
> Some drink because 'tis wet,
> And some because 'tis dry;
> Some drink another glass
> To wet the other eye.

Water is this gentleman's abhorrence, whether used inside or out, but most of all he dreads it taken inwardly, except with spirits, and then the less the better. He says that the pump would kill him, but he never gives it a chance. He laps his liquor, and licks his chaps, but he will never die through the badness of the water from the well. It is a pity that he does not run the risk. Drinking cold water neither makes a man sick, nor in debt, nor his wife a widow, but this mighty fine ale of his will do all this for him, make him worse than a beast while he lives, and wash him away to his grave before his time. The old Scotchman said, "Death and drink-draining are near neighbours," and he spoke the truth. They say that drunkenness makes some men fools, some beasts, and some devils, but according to my mind it makes all men fools whatever else it does. Yet when a man is as drunk as a rat he sets up to be a judge, and mocks at sober people. Certain neighbours of mine laugh at me for being a teetotaller, and I might well laugh at them for being drunk, only I feel more inclined to cry that they should be such fools. O that we could get them sober, and then perhaps we might make men of them. You cannot do much with these fellows, unless you can enlist them in the Coldstream guards.

> He that any good would win
> At his mouth must first begin.

As long as drink drowns conscience and reason, you might as well talk to the hogs. The rascals will promise fair and take the pledge, and then take their coats to pledge to get more beer. We smile at a tipsy man, for he is a ridiculous creature, but when we see how he is ruined body and soul it is no joking matter. How solemn is the truth that "No drunkard shall inherit eternal life."

There's nothing too bad for a man to say or do when he is half-seas over. It is a pity that any decent body should go near such a common sewer. If he does not fall into the worst of crimes it certainly is not his fault, for he has made himself ready for anything the devil likes to put into his mind. He does least hurt when he begins to be topheavy, and to reel about: then he becomes a blind man with good eyes in his head, and a cripple with legs on. He sees two moons, and two doors to the public-house, and tries to find his way through both the doors at once. Over he goes, and there he must lie unless somebody will wheel him home in a barrow or carry him to the police-station.

Solomon says the glutton and the drunkard shall come to poverty, and that the drinker does in no time. He gets more and more down at the heel, and as his nose gets redder and his body is more swollen he gets to be more of a shack and more of a shark. His trade is gone, and his credit has run out, but he still manages to get his beer. He treats an old friend to a pot, and then finds that he has left his purse at home, and of course the old friend must pay the shot. He borrows till no one will lend him a groat, unless it is to get off lending a shilling. Shame has long since left him, though all who know him are ashamed of him. His talk runs like the tap, and is full of stale dregs: he is very kind over his beer, and swears he loves you, and would like to drink your health, and love you again. Poor sot, much good will his blessing do to any one who gets it; his poor wife and family have had too much of it already, and quake at the very sound of his voice.

Now, if we try to do anything to shut up a boozing-house, or shorten the hours for guzzling, we are called all sorts of bad names, and the wind-up of it all is – *"What! Rob a poor man of his beer?"* The fact is that they rob the poor man *by* his beer. The ale-jug robs the cupboard and the table, starves the wife and strips the children; it is a great thief, housebreaker, and heartbreaker, and the best possible thing is to break it to pieces, or keep it on the shelf bottom upwards. In a newspaper which was lent me the other day I saw some verses by John Barleycorn, jun., and as they tickled my fancy I copied them out, and here they are.

> What! rob a poor man of his beer,
> And give him good victuals instead!
> Your heart's very hard, sir, I fear,
> Or at least you are soft in the head.

What! rob a poor man of his mug,
And give him a house of his own;
With kitchen and parlour so snug!
'Tis enough to draw tears from a stone.

What! rob a poor man of his glass,
And teach him to read and to write!
What! save him from being an ass!
'Tis nothing but malice and spite.

What! rob a poor man of his ale,
And prevent him from beating his wife,
From being locked up in a jail,
With penal employment for life!

What! rob a poor man of his beer,
And keep him from starving his child!
It makes one feel awfully queer,
And I'll thank you to draw it more mild.

Having given you a song, I now hand you a handbill to stick up in the "Rose and Crown" window, if the landlord wants an advertisement. It was written many years ago, but it is quite as good as new. Any beer-seller may print it who thinks it likely to help his trade (overleaf).

DRUNKARDS, READ THIS!

DRUNKENNESS

expels reason,
distempers the body,
diminishes strength,
inflames the blood;
causes internal wounds
causes external wounds
causes eternal wounds
cause incurable wounds
is
a witch to the senses,
a demon to the soul,
a thief to the purse,
a guide to beggary, lechery, & villainy.
it is
the wife's woe, and
the children's sorrow.
makes a man
wallow worse than a beast, and
act like a fool
He is
a self-murderer;
who drinks to another's good health,
and
robs himself of his own.

10
Every man should sweep before his own door.

He is a wise man who has wit enough for his own affairs. It is a common thing for people to *mind* Number One, but not so common to see people *mend* it. When it comes to spending money on labour or improvements, they think that repairs should begin at

Number 2, and Number 3, and go on till all the houses up to Number 50 are touched up before any hint should be given to Number One. Now, this is very stupid, for if charity should begin at home, certainly reformation should begin there too. It is a waste of time to go far away to make a clearance, there's nothing like sweeping the snow from your own door. Let every dog carry his own tail. Mind your own business, and mend your own manners, and if every man does the same all will be minded and mended, as the old song says:

> "Should every man defend his house,
> Then all would be defended;
> If every man would mend a man,
> Then all mankind were mended."

A man who does not look well to his own concerns is not fit to be trusted with other people's. Lots of folks are so busy abroad that they have no time to look at home. They say the cobbler's wife goes barefoot, and the baker's child gets no buns, and the sweep's house has sooty chimneys. This comes of a man's thinking that he is everybody except himself. All the wit in the world is not in one head, and therefore the wisest man living is not bound to look after all his neighbours' matters. There are wonderful people about whose wisdom would beat Solomon into fits; and yet they have not sense enough to keep their own kettle from boiling over. They could manage the nation, and yet can't keep their boys out of the farmer's orchard; they could teach the parson, but they can't learn themselves. They poke their noses into other people's concerns, where they are as welcome as water in one's shoes, but as for setting their own house to rights, they like the job about as much as a pig likes having a ring put in his nose. The meddlesome man will not begin to darn his own stockings because he has left his needle sticking in his cousin's socks: he will be as grey as grannum's cat before he improves, and yet he struts like a crow in a gutter, and thinks himself cock of the walk.

A man's own selfishness and conceit ought to make him see to his own ways if nothing else does.

> There's but one wise man in the world,
> And who d'ye think it be?
> 'Tis this man, that man, t'other man,
> Every man think's 'tis he.

Now, if this be so, why does not this wise man do the wise thing and set his own wise self in the way of growing wiser? Every cat cleans its own fur, and licks its own kittens: when will men and women mind their own minds, and busy themselves with their own business? Boil your own potatoes, and let me roast mine if I like; I won't do it with your firing. "Every man to his tent" was the old cry in Israel, and it's not a bad one for England, only Nelson gave us a better —

ENGLAND EXPECTS EVERY MAN
TO DO HIS DUTY.

11

Scant feeding of man or horse
is small profit and sure loss.

What is saved out of the food of cattle is a dead loss, for a horse can't work if he is not fed. If an animal won't pay for keeping he won't pay for starving. Even the land yields little if it is not nourished, and it is just the same with the poor beast. You might as well try to run a steam-engine without coals, or drive a water-mill without water, as work a horse without putting corn into him. Thomas Tusser, who wrote a book upon "Husbandry" in the olden time, said,

> "Who starveth his cattle, and weareth them out
> By carting and ploughing, his gain I much doubt:
> But he that in labour doth use them aright
> Has gain to his comfort, and cattle in plight."

Poor dumb animals cannot speak for themselves, and therefore every one who has his speech should plead for them. To keep them short of victuals is a crying shame. The one in our picture seems to be thoroughly broken in: look at his knees! His owner ought to be flogged at the cart tail. I hate cruelty, and above all things the cruelty which starves the labouring beast.

> A right good man is good to all,
> And stints not table, rack, or stall;
> Not only cares for horse and hog,
> But kindly thinks of cat and dog.

Is not a man better than a beast? Then, depend upon it, what is good for the ploughing horse is good for the ploughing boy: a belly full of plain food is a wonderful help to a labouring man. A starving workman is a dear servant. If you don't pay your men, they pay themselves, or else they shirk their work. He who labours well should be fed well, especially a ploughman.

> "Let such have enow
> That follow the plough."

There would be no bread if it were not for the ploughman: would you starve the man who is the very bottom and beginning of everything? John never brags, but he thinks well of his calling, and thinks well of those who pay well: as for those who grind the faces of the poor, the more John thinks of them the less he thinks of them. A man may live upon little, but Farmer Gripper thinks we can live upon nothing, which is a horse of another colour. I can't make out why the land cannot afford to keep those who work on it, for it used to do so. Tom Tusser wrote three hundred years ago,

> "Good ploughmen look weekly, of custom and right,
> For roast meat on Sundays, and Thursdays at night.
> Thus doing and keeping such custom and guise,
> They call thee good huswife, they love thee likewise."

This is what he writes to the farmer's wife about the ploughmen who lived at the farm house, but he has a bit to say for the other fellows and their privileges. About the harvest supper he says,

> "In harvest time, harvest folk, servants, and all,
> Should make all together good cheer in the hall."

I wish they would, but then they are so apt to drink. Could we not have a feast without the beer and headaches? This is old Tom's writing about the harvest supper, and so on,

> "For all this good feasting, yet art thou not loose,
> Till ploughman thou givest his harvest home goose.
> Though goose go in stubble, I pass not for that,
> Let Giles have a goose, be she lean, be she fat."

I fancy I see old Gripper giving Giles a goose: he would think Giles a green goose if he were to hint at it. Gripper is a close shaver; where he grazes no goose could pick up a living after him. He does not know what his lean labourers say of him, but he might guess, for a hungry man is an angry man, and an empty belly makes no compliments. As for lazy fellows who will eat till they sweat and work till they freeze, I don't mind what short commons they get; but a real hard-working man ought to be able to get for a day's work enough to keep himself and family from hunger. If this cannot be done, something is wrong somewhere, as the man said when he sat down on a setting of eggs. I am not going to blame the farmers, or the landlords, or the Parliament men, or anybody; but the land is good, and yields plenty for man and beast, and neither horse nor man should be starved.

There is no gain in being niggardly to your cattle. I have known men buy old screws of horses and feed them badly, and yet pay more in the long run for ploughing than the owner of a good team who gave out a fair allowance. The poor things can't work if they don't eat. As I said before, I speak up for the horses because they can't speak for themselves. All they *can* say, however, goes to prove what I have written: ask them if they can plough well when they get bad corn, and little of it, and they answer with a neigh.

As for the men, I wish they were, all round, a more deserving set, but I am obliged to own that many are better at grubbing than ploughing. I would say to them, "Do good work, and then ask for good wages." I am afraid that many are not worth more than they get. Our old master used to say to Crawley Jones —

211

> "You feed so fast, and walk so very slow —
> Eat with your legs, and with your grinders go."

But then, if Jones was a slow man, he certainly had slow pay. He did not see the fun of working to the tune of twenty shillings when he had only ten. If he had done more master would have given him more, but Jones couldn't see that, and so he mouched about, doing next to nothing, and got next to nothing for it. He very seldom got a bit of meat, and there was no bone or muscle in the man. He seemed to be fed on turnip-tops, and was as dull as a dormouse in winter time, and unless you had emptied a skip of bees over him you couldn't have woke him up. They say that Johnny Raw is a stupid; he would not be half so stupid if he had more *raw* to put in his pot.

> Though lubbers might loiter with belly too full,
> We're not in that case, but our belts we must pull;
> Could we manage to get a little more meat,
> We could do twice as much, and think it no feat.

They call a ploughman Chaw-bacon, do they? Wouldn't he like a bit more bacon to chaw? Hundreds and thousands of hard-working men down in the shires hardly get enough fat to grease the wheels of life, and the more's the pity. As to the poor women and children, it is often short-cake with them: bread, and pull it, and little of that.

One thing, however, is as plain as a pike-staff: the labourer cannot afford to keep a public house going while he has so little for his own private house. He has not a penny to spare, I'm sure, but had need to take all home to the missus that he can make by hook or by crook. Miss

Hannah More wrote two verses which every ploughman should read, and mark, and learn.

> "We say the times are grievous hard,
> And hard they are, 'tis true!
> But, drinkers, to your wives and babes
> They're harder made by you.
>
> "The drunkard's tax is self-imposed,
> Like every other sin;
> The taxes altogether cost
> Not half so much as gin."

Well, if after all our being sober and thrifty, we cannot get along without pinching, let us still be patient and contented. We have more blessings than we can count even now. If masters happen to be close-fisted, God is open-handed, and if the outward food be scant, the bread of heaven is plentiful. Cheer up, brother ploughman, it's better on before. There is a city where "the very streets are paved with gold exceeding clear and fine." This should make us feel like singing all the time, and help us to follow the advice of old Thomas —

> "At bed, and at board, whatsoever befall,
> Whatever God sendeth, be merry withal."

12
Never stop the plough to catch a mouse.

There's not much profit in this game. Think of a man and a boy and four horses all standing still for the sake of a mouse! What would old friend Tusser say to that? I think he would rhyme in this fashion –

A ploughman deserveth a cut of the whip
If for idle pretence he let the hours slip.

Heaps of people act like the man in our picture. They have a great work in hand which wants all their wits, and they leave it to squabble over some pretty nothing, not worth a fig. Old master Tom would say to them —

No more tittle tattle, go on with your cattle.

He could not bear for a farmer to let his horses out for carting even, because it took their work away from the farm, and so I am sure he would be in a great stew if he saw farmers wasting their time at matches, and hunts, and the like. He says —

"Who slacketh his tillage a carter to be,
For groat got abroad, at home shall lose three;
For sure by so doing he brings out of heart,
  Both land for the corn, and horse for the cart."

The main chance must be minded, and the little things must be borne with. Nobody would burn his house down to kill the blackbeetles, and it would never answer to kill the bullocks to feed the cats. If our baker left off making bread for a week while he cracked the cockroaches, what should we all do for breakfast? If the butcher sold no more meat till he had killed all the blow-flies, we should be many a day without mutton. If the water companies never gave the Londoners a drink till they had fished every gudgeon out of the Thames, how would the old ladies make their tea? There's no use in stopping your fishing because of the sea-weed, nor your riding because of the dust.

Now, our minister said to me the other day, "John, if you were on the committees of some of our societies you would see this mouse-hunting done to perfection. Not only committees, but whole bodies of Christian people, go mouse-hunting." Well, said I, minister, just write me a bit, and I will stick it in my book, it will be beef to my horse-radish. Here's his writing—

> "A society of good Christian people will split into pieces over a petty quarrel, or mere matter of opinion, while all around them the masses are perishing for want of the gospel. A miserable little mouse, which no cat would ever hunt, takes them off from their Lord's work. Again, intelligent men will spend months of time and heaps of money in inventing and publishing mere speculations, while the great field of the world lies unploughed. They seem to care nothing how many may perish so long as they can ride their hobbies. In other matters a little common sense is allowed to rule, but in the weightiest matters foolishness is sadly conspicuous. As for you and me, John, let us kill a mouse when it nibbles our bread, but let us not spend our lives over it. What can be done by a mousetrap or a cat should not occupy all our thoughts.
>
> The paltry trifles of this world are much of the same sort. Let us give our chief attention to the chief things, - the glory of God, the winning of souls for Jesus, and our own salvation. There are fools enough in the world, and there can be no need that Christian men should swell the number. Go on with your ploughing, John, and I will go on with my preaching, and in due season we shall reap if we faint not."

13
A looking-glass is no use to a blind man.

He who will not see is much the same as if he had no eyes; indeed, in some things, the man without eyes has the advantage, for he is in the dark *and knows it*. A lantern is of no use to a bat, and good teaching is lost on the man who will not learn. Reason is folly with the unreasonable. One man can lead a horse to the water, but a hundred cannot make him drink: it is easy work to tell a man the truth, but if he will not be convinced your labour is lost. We pity the poor blind, we cannot do so much as that for those who shut their eyes against the light.

A man who is blind to his own faults is blind to his own interests. He who thinks that he never was a fool is a fool now. He who never owns that he is wrong will never get right. He'll mend, as the saying is, when he grows better, like sour beer in summer. How can a man take the smuts off his face if he will not look in the glass, nor believe that they are there when he is told of them?

Prejudice shuts up many eyes in total darkness. The man knows already: he is positive and can swear to it, and it's no use your arguing. He has made up his mind, and it did not take him long, for there's very little of it, but when he has said a thing he sticks to it like cobbler's wax. He is wiser than seven men that can render a reason. He is as positive as if he had been on the other side of the curtain and looked into the back yard of the universe. He talks as if he carried all knowledge in his waistcoat pocket, like a peppermint lozenge. Those who like may try to teach him, but I don't care to hold up a mirror to a mole.

Some men are blinded by their worldly business, and could not see heaven itself if the windows were open over their heads. Look at farmer Grab, he is like Nebuchadnezzar, for his conversation is all among beasts, and if he does not eat grass it is because he never could stomach salads. His dinner is his best devotion, he is a terrible fastener on a piece of beef, and sweats at it more than at his labour. As old Master Earle says, "His religion is a part of his copyhold, which he takes from his landlord, and refers wholly to his lordship's discretion. If he gives him leave, he goes to church in his best clothes, and sits there with his neighbours, but never prays more than two prayers – for rain and for fair weather, as the case may be. He is a niggard all the week, except on market days, where, if his corn sell well, he thinks he may be drunk with a good conscience. He is sensible of no calamity but the burning of a stack of corn, or the overflowing of a meadow, and he thinks Noah's flood the greatest plague that ever was, not because it drowned the world, but spoiled the grass. For death he is never troubled, and if he gets in his harvest before it happens, it may come when it will, he cares not." He is as stubborn as he is stupid, and to get a new thought into his head you would need to bore a hole in his skull with a centre-bit. The game would not be worth the candle. We must leave him alone, for he is too old in the tooth, and too blind to be made to see.

Other people hurt their eyes by using glasses which are not spectacles. I have tried to convince Joe Scroggs that it would be a fine thing for him to join the teetotallers, and he has nothing to say against it only "he does not see it."

> "He up and told me to my face,
> The chimney corner should be his place,
> And there he'd sit and dye his face,
> And drink till all is blue."

All is blue with him now, for his furniture is nearly all sold, and his wife and children have not a shoe to their foot, and yet he laughs about "a yard of pump water," and tells me to go and drink my cocoa. Poor soul! Poor soul!

> In tippling is his sole delight,
> Each sign-post bars his way;
> He spends in muddy ale at night
> The wages of the day.

Can nothing be done for such poor fools. Why not shorten the hours for dealing out the drink? Why not shut up the public-houses on Sundays? If these people have not got sense enough to take care of themselves the law should protect them. Will Shepherd says he has to fetch his sheep out of a field when they are likely to get blown through eating too much green meat, and there ought to be power to fetch sots out of a beer-shop when they are worse than blowed through drink. How I wish I could make poor Scroggs see as I do, but there, if a fellow has no eyes he can't see the sun, though his nose is being scorched off in the glare of it.

Of all dust the worst for the eyes is gold dust. A bribe blinds the judgment, and riches darken the mind. As smoke to the eyes, so also is flattery to the soul, and prejudice turns the light of the sun into a darkness that may be felt. We are all blind by nature, and till the good Physician opens our eyes we grope, even in gospel light. All the preaching in the world cannot make a man see the truth so long as his eyes are blinded. There is a heavenly eye-salve which is a sovereign cure, but the worst of the matter is that the blind in heart think they see already, and so they are likely to die in darkness. Let us pray for those who never pray for themselves: God's power can do for them what is far beyond our power.

> A dark and blinded thing is man,
> Yet full of fancied light!
> But all his penetration can
> Obtain no gospel light.
>
> Though heavenly truth may blaze abroad
> He cannot see at all;
> Though gospel leaders show the road,
> He still gropes for the wall.
>
> Perhaps he stands to hear the sound,
> But blind he still remains,
> No meaning in the word is found
> To cause him joys or pains.
>
> O Lord, thy holy power display,
> For thou the help must find;
> Pour in the light of gospel day,
> Illuminate the blind.
>
> Behold, how unconcerned they dwell
> Though reft of sight they be,
> They fancy they can see right well,
> And need no help from thee.
>
> Speak, and they'll mourn for their blinded eyes,
> And cry to thee for light;
> O Lord, do not our prayer despise,
> But give these blind men sight.

14

He has got the fiddle, but not the stick.

It often comes to pass that a man steps into another's shoes, and yet cannot walk in them. A poor tool of a parson gets into a good man's pulpit, and takes the same texts, but the sermons are chalk, and not cheese.

A half-baked young swell inherits his father's money but not his generosity, his barns but not his brains, his title but not his sense, - he has the fiddle without the stick, and more's the pity.

Some people imagine that they have only to get hold of the plough-handles, and they would soon beat John Ploughman. If they had his fiddle they are sure they could play on it. J. P. presents his compliments, and wishes he may be there when it is done.

> "That I fain would see,
> Quoth blind George of Hollowee."

However, between you and me and the bedpost, there is one secret which John does not mind letting out. John's fiddle is poor enough, but the stick is a right good one, too good to be called a fiddle-stick. Do you want to see the stick with which John plays his fiddle? Here it is — Looking to God for help, John always tries to do his best, whatever he has to do, and he has found this to be the very best way to play all kinds of tunes. What little music there is in John's poor old fiddle comes out of it in that way. Listen to a scrape or two.

> If I were a cobbler, I'd make it my pride
> The best of all cobblers to be;
> If I were a tinker, no tinker beside
> Should mend an old kettle like me.

> And being a ploughman, I plough with the best,
> No furrow runs straighter than mine;
> I waste not a moment, and stay not to rest,
> Though idlers to tempt me combine.

Yet I wish not to boast, for trust I have none
In aught I can do or can be;
I rest in my Saviour, and what he has done
To ransom poor sinners like me.

15
"Great cry and little wool,"
as the man said who clipped the sow.

Our friend Hodge does not seem to be making much of an out at shearing. It will take him all his time to get wool enough for a blanket, and his neighbours are telling him so, but he does not heed them, for a man never listens to reason when he has made up his mind to act unreasonably. Hodge gets plenty of music of a sort: Hullah's system is nothing to it, and even Nebuchadnezzar's flutes, harps, sackbuts, and dulcimers could not make more din. He gets "cry" enough to stock a Babylon of babies, but not wool enough to stop his ears with.

Now, is not this very like the world with its notions of pleasure? There is noise enough; laughter and shouting, and boasting; but where is the comfort which can warm the heart and give peace to the spirit? Generally there's plenty of smoke and very little fire in what is called pleasure. It promises a nag and gives an egg. Gaiety is a sort of flash in the pan, a fifth of November squib, all fizz and bang and done for. The devil's meal is all bran, and the world's wine turns to vinegar. It is always making a great noise over nutshells. Thousands have had to weep over their blunder in looking for their heaven on earth; but they follow each other like sheep through a gap, not a bit the wiser for the experience of generations. It seems that every man must have a clip at his own particular pig, and cannot be made to believe that like all the rest it will yield him nothing but bristles. Men are not all of one mind as to what is best for them; they no more agree than the clocks in our village, but they all hang together in following after vanity, for to the core of their hearts they are vain.

One shears the publican's hog, which is so fond of the swill tub, and he reckons upon bringing home a wonderful lot of wool; but everybody knows that he who goes to the "Woolpack" for wool will come home shorn: the "Blue

Boar" is an uncommonly ugly animal to shear, and so is the "Red Lion." Better sheer off as fast as you can; it will be sheer folly to stop. You may loaf about the tap of the "Halfmoon" till you get the full moon in your noddle, and need a keeper: it is the place for men whose wits go woolgathering, but wool there is none.

Another is covetous, and hopes to escape misery by being a miser: his greedy mind can no more be filled than a lawyer's purse: he never has enough, and so he never has a feast. He makes money with his teeth, by keeping them idle. That is a very lean hog to clip at, for poverty wants some things, luxury many things, but covetousness wants all things. If we could hoard up all the money in the world, what would it be to us at last? Today at good cheer, tomorrow on the bier: in the midst of life we are in death.

Some, like old Mrs Too-good, go in for self-righteousness, and their own mouths dub them saints. They are the pink of perfection, the cream of creation, the gems of their generation, and yet a sensible man would not live in the same house with them for all the money you could count. They are saints abroad, but ask their maids what they are at home. Great cry and little wool is common enough in religion: you will find that those who crack themselves up are generally cracked, and those who despise their neighbours come to be despised themselves.

Many try wickedness, and run into bad company, and rake the kennels of vice. I warrant you they may shear the whole styful of filthy creatures and never find a morsel of wool on the whole lot of them. Loose characters, silly amusements, gambling, wantonness, and such like, are swine that none but a fool will try his shears upon. I don't deny that there's plenty of swinish music — who ever expected that there would be silence in a piggery? But then noise cannot fill the heart, nor laughter lighten the soul.

John Ploughman has tried for himself, and he knows by experience that all the world is nothing but a hog that is not worth the shearing: "Vanity of vanities, all is vanity." But yet there is wool to be had; there are real joys to be got for the asking if we ask aright. Below, all things deceive us, but above us there is a true Friend. "Wherefore do ye spend your money for that which is not bread, and your labour for that which satisfieth not?" This is John Ploughman's verdict, which he wishes all his readers to take note of —

> "Faith in Jesus Christ will give
> Sweetest pleasures while we live;
> Faith in Jesus must supply
> Solid comfort when we die."

16
You may bend the sapling,
but not the tree.

Ladder, and pole, and cord will be of no use to straighten the bent tree; it should have been looked after much earlier. Train trees when they are saplings and young lads before the down comes on their chins. If you want a bullfinch to pipe, whistle to him while he is young; he will scarcely catch the tune after he has learnt the wild bird's note. Begin early to teach, for children begin early to sin. Catch them young and you may hope to keep them.

> Ere your boy has reached to seven,
> Teach him well the way to heaven;
> Better still the work will thrive,
> If he learns before he's five.

What is learned young is learned for life. What we hear at the first we remember to the last. The bent twig grows up a crooked tree. Horse-breakers say

> "The tricks a colt getteth at his first backing
> Will whilst he continueth never be lacking."

When a boy is rebellious, conquer him, and do it well the first time, that there may be no need to do it again. A child's first lesson should be obedience, and after that you may teach it what you please: yet the young mind must not be laced too tight, or you may hurt its growth and hinder its strength. They say a daft nurse makes a wise child, but I do not believe it: nobody needs so much common sense as a mother or a governess. It does not do to be always thwarting; and yet remember if you give a child his will and a whelp his fill, both will surely turn out ill. A child's back must be made to bend, but it must not be broken. He must be ruled, but not with a rod of iron. His spirit must be conquered, but not crushed.

Nature does sometimes overcome nurture, but for the most part the teacher wins the day. Children are what they are made: the pity is that so many are spoiled in the bringing up. A child may be rocked too hard; you may spoil him either by too much cuffing or too much kissing. I knew two boys who had a Christian mother, but she always let them have their own way. The consequence was that when they grew up they took to drinking and low company and soon spent the fortune their father left them. No one controlled them and they had no control over themselves, and so they just rattled along the broad road like butcher boys with runaway horses, and there was no stopping them. A birch or two worn out upon them when they were little would have been a good use of timber.

Still, a child can be treated too hardly, and especially he can be shut up too many hours in school, when a good run and a game of play would do him more good. Cows don't give any the more milk for being often milked, nor do children learn any more because of very long hours in a hot room.

A boy can be driven to learn till he loses half his wits: forced fruits have little flavour; a man at five is a fool at fifteen. If you make veal of the calf he will never turn to beef. Yet learning may be left so long that the little dunce is always behindhand.

There's a medium in everything and he is a good father who hits upon it, so that he governs his family with love, and his family loves to be governed by him. Some are like Eli, who let his sons sin and only chided them a little; these will turn out to be cruel parents in the long run: others are too strict, and make home miserable, and so drive the youngsters to the wrong road in another way. Tight clothes are very apt to tear, and hard laws are often broken: but loose garments tear too, and where there are no laws at all, things are sure to go amiss. So you see it is easy to err on either side, and hard to dance the tight-rope of wisdom. Depend on it, he who has a wife and bairns will never be short of care to carry. See what we get when we come to marry, yet many there are who will not tarry.

In these days children have a deal too much of their own way, and often make their mothers and fathers their slaves. It has come to a fine pass when the goslings teach the geese, and the kittens rule the cat: it is the upsetting of everything, and no parent ought to put up with it. It is as bad for the boys and girls as it is for the grown folks, and it brings out the worst side of their characters. I would sooner be a cat on hot bricks, or a toad under a harrow, than let my own children be my masters. No, the head must be the head, or it will hurt the whole body.

> For children out place
> Are a father's disgrace,
> If you rule not you'll rue,
> For they'll quickly rule you.

17
A man may love his house,
though he ride not on the ridge.

Y ou can love your house and not ride on the ridge;
there's a medium in everything. You can be fond of
your wife without being her drudge, and you can love your
children dearly, and yet not give them their own way in

everything. Some men are of so strange a kidney that they set no bounds to their nonsense. If they are fond of roast beef they must needs suck the spit; they cannot rest with eating the pudding, they must swallow the bag. If they dislike a thing, the very smell of it sets them grumbling, and if they like it they must have it everywhere and always, for nothing else is half so sweet. When they do go in for eating rabbits, they have

> Rabbits young and rabbits old,
> Rabbits hot and rabbits cold,
> Rabbits tender, rabbits tough:
> Never can they have enough.

Whatever they take up takes them up, and for a season they cannot seize on anything else. At election times the barber cannot trim his customer's poll because of the polling, and the draper cannot serve you with calico because he is canvassing. The nation would go to the dogs altogether if the cat's-meat man did not secure the election by sticking his mark on the ballot paper. It is supposed that the globe would leave off turning round if our Joe Scroggs did not go down to the "Dun Cow," and read the paper, and have his say upon politics, in the presence of the house of commons assembled in the taproom. I do not quite think so, but I know this, that when the Whigs and the Tories and the Radicals are about, Scroggs is good for nothing all day long. What party he belongs to I don't know, but I believe his leading principle will be seen in the following verse—

> If gentlemen propose a glass
> He never says them nay;

For he always thinks it right to drink
While other people pay.

You can make a good thing become a nuisance by harping on that one string from dawn to dusk. A hen with one chick makes no end of scratching and clucking, and so does a fellow of one idea. He has a bee in his bonnet, and he tries to put a wasp in yours. He duns you, and if you do not agree with him he counts you his enemy. When you meet with him you are unfortunate, and when you leave him you will better yourself go where you may: "there's small sorrow at our parting," as the old mare said to the broken cart. You may try to humour him, but he will have all the more humours if you do, for the man knows no moderation, and if you let him ride on the roof he will soon sit on the chimney-pot.

One man of my acquaintance used to take Morrison's pills every day of his life, and when I called in to see him I had not been there ten minutes before he wanted me to take a dose, but I could not swallow what he told me nor the pills either, so I told him I dare say they were very good for him, but they did not suit my constitution: however, he kept on with his subject till I was fain to be off. Another man never catches sight of me but he talks about vaccination and goes on against it till he froths at the mouth, and I am half afraid he will inoculate me. My master had a capital horse, worth a good deal of money, only he always shied at a stone-heap on the road, and if there were fifty of them he always bolted off the road every time. He had got heaps on his brain, poor creature, and though he was fit for a nobleman's carriage he had to be put to plough. Some men have got stone-heaps in their poor noddles and this spoils them for life and makes it dangerous for all who have to deal with them. What queer fish there are in our pond! I am afraid that most of us have a crack somewhere, but we don't all show it quite so much as some. We ought to have a good deal of patience, and then we shall find amusement where else we should be bothered to death. One of my mates says the world is not round, and so I always drop into his notion and tell him this is a flat world and he is a flat too.

What a trial it is to be shut up for an hour with a man or a woman with a hobby; riding in a horse-box with a bear with a sore head is nothing to it. The man is so fond of bacon that he wants you to kiss his pig, and all the while you hope you will never again see either the man or his pork as long as you live. No matter what the whole hog may be, the man who goes it is terrible.

> Rocking horse for boy,
> Hobby horse for man;
> Each one rides his toy
> Whenever he can.
>
> The boy is right glad
> Though he rideth alone;
> His father's own fad
> By the world must be known.
>
> Of the two hobby rides,
> The boy's is the best;
> For the man often chides,
> And gives you no rest.

It is a good thing for a man to be fond of his own trade and his own place, but still there is reason in everything, even in roasting eggs. When a man thinks that his place is below him he will pretty soon be below his place, and therefore a good opinion of your own calling is by no means an evil; yet nobody is everybody, and no trade is to crow over the rest. The cobbler has his awl but he is not all, and the hatter wears a crown but he is not king. A man may come to market without buying my onions, and ploughing can be done with other horses than mine, though Dapper and Violet are something to brag of. The farming interest is no doubt first, and so is the saddler's, and so is the tinker's, and so is the grocer's, and so is the draper's, and so is the parson's, and so is the parish beadle's, and so is every other interest according to each man's talk.

> Your trade, as a trade, is all very well,
> But other good folk have their cheeses to sell;
> You must not expect all the world to bow down,
> And give to one pedlar the sceptre and crown.

It is astonishing how much men will cry up small matters. They are very busy, but it is with catching flies. They talk about a mushroom till you would think it was the only thing at the Lord Mayor's dinner, and the beef and the turkeys went for nothing. They say nothing about the leg of mutton, for they are so much in love with the trimmings. They can't keep things in their places, but make more of a horse's tail than they do of his whole body. Like the cock on the dunghill, they consider a poor barley-corn to be worth more than a diamond. A thing happens to suit their taste and so there is nothing like it in the whole of England; no, nor in all America or Australia. A duck will not always dabble in the same gutter, but they will; for, bless your heart, they don't think it a gutter, but a river, if not an ocean. They must ride the ridge of the roof, or else burn the house down. A good many people love their dogs, but these folks take them to bed with them. Other farmers fat the calf, but they fall down and worship it, and what is worse they quarrel with everybody who does not think as much of their idol as they do.

It will be a long while before all men become wise, but it will help on the time if we begin to be wise ourselves. Don't let us make too much of this world and the things of it. We are to use it but not to abuse it; to live *in* it but not *for* it; to love our house but not to *ride* on the ridge. Our daily bread and daily work are to be minded, and yet we must not mind earthly things. We must not let the body send the soul to grass, rather must we make the limbs servants to the soul. The world must not rule us, we must reign as kings though we are only ploughmen; and stand upright even if the world be turned upside down.

18
Great drinkers think themselves great men.

Wonderful men and white rats are not so scarce as most people think. Folks may talk as they like about Mr. Gladstone and Lord Beaconsfield, and that sharp gentleman Bismarck, but Jack, and Tom, and

Harry, and scores more that I know of, could manage their business for them a fine sight better; at least, they think so, and are quite ready to try. Great men are as plentiful as mice in an old wheat-stack down our way. Every parish has one or two wonderful men; indeed, most public-houses could show one at least, and generally two; and I have heard that on Saturday nights, when our "Blue Dragon" is full, there may be seen as many as twenty of the greatest men in all the world in the taproom, all making themselves greater by the help of pots of beer. When the jug has been filled and emptied a good many times, the blacksmith feels he ought to be prime minister; Styles, the carter, sees the way to take off all the taxes, and Old Hob, the rat-catcher, roars out —

> "They're all a pack of fools,
> And good-for-nothing tools;
> If they'd only send for me,
> You'd see how things would be."

If you have a fancy to listen to these great men when they are talking you need not go into the bar, for you can hear them outside the house; they generally speak four or five at a time, and every one in a Mitcham whisper, which is very like a shout. What a fine flow of words they have! There's no end to it, and it's a pity there was ever any beginning, for there's generally a mix up of foul talk with their politics, and this sets them all roaring with laughter. A few evenings in such company would poison the mind of the best lad in the parish. I am happy to say that these great men have to be turned out at ten o'clock, for then our public-house closes; and none too soon, I'm sure.

A precious little is enough to make a man famous in certain companies; one fellow knocked a man's eye out at a prize-fight; another stowed away twice as much pudding as four pigs could have disposed of; another stood on his head and drank a glass of beer; and another won a prize by grinning through a horse-collar; and for such things as these the sots of the village think mightily of them. Little things please little minds, and nasty things please dirty minds. If I were one of these wonderful fellows I would ask the nearest way to a place where nobody would know me.

Now I am at it, I will notice a few other wonderful bodies who sometimes condescend to look down on a ploughman; but before I make them angry I would give them a verse from one of my old uncle's songs, which I have shaped a bit.

> "I hope none will be offended with me for writing this,
> For it is not intended for anything amiss;
> If you consider kindly my remarks you will allow,
> For what can you expect from one whose hand is on
> the plough?"

I used to feel quite staggered when I heard of an amazing clever man, but I've got used to it, as the rook did to the scarecrow when he found out that it was a stuffed nothing. Like the picture which looked best at a very long distance off, so do most clever fellows. They are swans a mile off, but geese when you get near them. Some men are too knowing to be wise, their boiler bursts because they have more steam than they can use. They know too much, and having gone over the top of the ladder they have gone down on the other side. People who are really wise never think themselves so: one of them said to me the other day, -

"All things I thought I knew; but now confess
The more I know I know I know the less."

Simple Simon is in a sad plight in such a world as this, but on the whole he gets on better than a fellow who is too clever by half. Every mouse had need have its eyes open nowadays, for the cats are very many and uncommonly sharp; and yet, you mark my word, most of the mice that are caught are the knowing ones. Somehow or other, in an ordinary sort of a world like this, it does not answer to be so over and above clever. Those who are up to so many dodges, find the dodges come down on them before long. My neighbour Hinks was much too wise a man to follow the plough, like poor shallow-pated John Ploughman, and so he took to scheming, and has schemed himself into one of the largest mansions in the country, where he will be provided with oakum to pick and a crank to turn during the next six calendar months. He had better have been a fool, for his cleverness has cost him his character.

When a man is too clever to tell the truth he will bring himself into no end of trouble before long. When he is too clever to stick to his trade, he is like the dog that let the meat fall into the water through trying to catch at its shadow. Clever Jack can do everything and can do nothing. He intends to be rich all at once, and despises small gains, and therefore is likely to die a beggar. When puffing is trusted and honest trading is scoffed at, time will not take long to wind up the concern. Work is as needful now as ever it was if a man would thrive; catching birds by putting salt on their tails would be all very well, but the creatures will not hold their tails still, and so we had better catch them in the usual way. The greatest trick for getting on in business is to work hard and to live hard. There's no making bread without flour, nor building houses without labour. I know the old saying is —

"No more mortar, no more brick,
A cunning knave has a cunning trick;"

but for all that things go on much the same as ever, and bricks and mortar are still wanted.

I see in the papers, every now and then, that some of the clever gentlemen who blow up bubble companies are pulled up before the courts. Serve them right! May they go where my neighbour Hinks is, every one of them. How many a poor tradesman is over head and ears in difficulty through them! I hope in future all men will fight shy of these fine companies, and swell managers, and very clever men. Men are neither suddenly rich nor suddenly good. It is all a bag of moonshine when a man would persuade you that he knows a way of earning money by winking your eye. We have all heard of the scheme for making deal boards out of sawdust, and getting butter out of mud, but we mean to go on with the saw-mill, and keep on milking the cows; for between you and me and the blind mare, we have a notion that the plans of idiots and very clever men are as like as two peas in a shell.

The worst sort of clever men are those who know better than the Bible and are so learned that they believe that the world had no Maker, and that men are only monkeys with their tails rubbed off. Dear, dear me, this is the sort of talk we used to expect from Tom of Bedlam, but now we get it from clever men. If things go on in this fashion a poor ploughman will not be able to tell which is the lunatic and which is the philosopher. As for me, the old Book seems to be a deal easier to believe than the new notions, and I mean to keep to it. Many a drop of good broth is made in an old pot, and many a sweet comfort comes out of the old doctrine. Many a dog has died since I first opened my eyes, and every one of these dogs has had his day, but in all the days put together they have never hunted out a real fault in the Bible, nor started anything better in its place. They may be very clever, but they will not find a surer truth than that which God teaches, nor a better salvation than that which Jesus brings, and so finding my very life in the gospel I mean to live in it, and so ends this chapter.

19
Two dogs fight for a bone,
and a third runs away with it.

We have all heard of the two men who quarrelled over an oyster, and called in a judge to settle the question: he ate the oyster himself, and gave them a shell each. This reminds me of the story of the cow which two farmers could not agree about, and so the lawyers stepped in and milked the cow for them, and charged them for their trouble in drinking the milk. Little is got by law, but much is lost by it. A suit in law may last longer than any suit a tailor can make you, and you may yourself be worn out before it comes to an end. It is better far to make matters up and keep out of court, for if you are caught there you are caught in the brambles, and won't get out without damage. John Ploughman feels a cold sweat at the thought of getting into the hands of lawyers. He does not mind going to Jericho, but he dreads the gentlemen on the road, for they seldom leave a feather upon any goose which they pick up.

However, if men will fight they must not blame the lawyers; if law were cheaper, quarrelsome people would have more of it, and quite as much would be spent in the long run. Sometimes, however, we get dragged into court willy nilly, and then one had need be wise as a serpent and harmless as a dove. Happy is he who finds an honest lawyer, and does not try to be his own client. A good lawyer always tries to keep people out of the law; but some clients are like moths with the candle, they must and will burn themselves. He who is so wise that he cannot be taught will have to pay for his pride.

> Let dogs delight to bark and bite,
> And lose the marrow bone;
> Let bears and lions growl and fight,
> I'll let the law alone.
> To suffer wrong is surely sad,
> But law-suits are in vain;
> To throw good money after bad
> Will but increase my pain.

20
He lives under the sign of the cat's foot.

I'M YOUR MATCH   I SCRATCH.

The question was once asked, When should a man marry? and the merry answer was, that for young men it is too soon and for old men it is too late. This is all very fine, but will not wash. Both the wisdom and the folly of men seem banded together to make a mock of this doctrine. Men are such fools that they must and will marry even if they marry fools. It is wise to marry when we can marry wisely, and then the sooner the better. How many show their sense in choosing a partner it is not for me to say, but I fear that in many cases love is blind, and makes a very blind choice. I don't suppose that some people would ever get married at all if love had its wits about it. It is a mystery how certain parties ever found partners; truly there's no accounting for tastes. However, as they make their bed they must lie on it, and as they tie the knot they must be tied by it. If a man catches a tartar, or lets a tartar catch him, he must take his dose of tartaric acid, and make as few ugly faces as he can. If a three-legged stool come flying through the air, he must be thankful for such a plain token of love from the woman of his choice, and the best thing he can do is to sit down on it, and wait for the next little article.

When it is said of a man, "He lives under the sign of the cat's foot," he must try and please his pussy that she may not scratch him more than such cats generally do. A good husband will generally have a good wife, or make a bad wife better. Bad Jack makes a great noise about bad Jill, but there's generally twenty of one where there's a score of the other. They say a burden of one's own choosing is never felt to be heavy, but I don't know, some men are loaded with mischief as soon as they have a wife to carry. Yet

> A good woman is worth, if she were sold,
> The fairest crown that's made of gold.

She is a pleasure, a treasure, and a joy without measure. A good wife and health are a man's best wealth; and he who is in such a case should envy no man's place. Even when a woman is a little tart it is better than if she had no spirit, and made her house into a dirt pie. A shrew is better than a slut, though one can be quite miserable enough with either. If she is a good housewife, and looks well after the children, one may put up with a Caudle lecture now and then, though a cordial lecture would be a deal better. A husband is in a pickle indeed if he gets tied up to a regular scold; he might as well be skinned and set up to his neck in a tub of brine. Did you ever hear the scold's song? Read it, you young folks who think of committing matrimony, and think twice before you get married once.

> When in the morn I open mine eyes
> To entertain the day,
> Before my husband e'en can rise,
> I scold him – then I pray.

> When I at table take my place,
> Whatever be the meat,
> I first do scold – and then say grace,
> If so disposed to eat.

> Too fat, too lean, too hot, too cold,
> I always do complain;
> Too raw, too roast, too young, too old –
> Faults I will find or feign.

> Let it be flesh, or fowl, or fish,
> It never shall be said,

> But I'll find fault with meat or dish,
> With master, or with maid.
>
> But when I go to bed at night
> I heartily do weep,
> That I must part with my delight –
> I cannot scold and sleep.
>
> However, this doth mitigate
> And much abate my sorrow,
> That though tonight it be too late,
> I'll early scold tomorrow.

When the husband is not a man it is not to be wondered at if the wife wears the top-boots: the mare may well be the best horse when the other horse is a donkey. Well may a woman feel that she is lord and master when she has to earn the living for the family, as is sometimes the case. She ought not to be the head, but if she has all the brains, what is she to do? What poor dawdles many men would be without their wives! As poor softy Simpkins says, if Bill's wife becomes a widow who will cut the pudding up for him, and will there be a pudding at all? It is grand when the wife knows her place, and keeps it, and they both pull together in everything. Then she is a helpmeet indeed and makes the house a home. Old friend Tusser says,

> "When husband is absent let housewife be chief,
> And look to their labour who live from their sheaf,
> The housewife's so named for she keepeth the house,
> And must tend on her profit as cat on a mouse."

He is very pat upon it that much of household affairs must rest on the wife, and he writes, -

"Both out, not allow,
Keep home, housewife thou."

Like the old man and woman in the toy which shows the weather, one must be sure to be in if the other goes out. When the king is abroad the queen must reign at home, and when he returns to his throne he is bound to look upon her as his crown, and prize her above gold and jewels. He should feel "if there's only one good wife in the whole world, I've got her." John Ploughman has long thought just that of his own wife, and after five-and-twenty years he is more sure of it than ever. He never bets, but he would not mind wagering a farthing cake that there is not a better woman on the surface of the globe than his own, very own beloved. Happy is the man who is happy in his wife. Let him love her as he loves himself, and a little better, for she is his better half.

Thank God that hath so blest thee,
And sit down, John, and rest thee.

There is one case in which I don't wonder if the wife does put her mate under the cat's foot, and that is when he slinks off to the public, and wastes his wages. Even then love and gentleness is the best way of getting him home; but, really, some topers have no feeling, and laugh at kindness, and therefore nobody can be surprised if the poor wife bristles up and gives her lord and master a taste of tongue. Nothing tries married love more than the pot-house. Wages wasted, wife neglected, children in rags: if she gives it him hot and strong who can blame her? Pitch into him, good woman, and make him ashamed of himself, if you can. No wonder that you lead a cat and dog life while he is such a sorry dog.

Still, you may as well go home and set him a better example, for two blacks will never make a white, and if you put him in hot water he's sure to get some spirits to mix with it.

21

He would put his finger in the pie,
so he burnt his nail off.

Some men must have a finger in every pie, or, as the proverb hath it, "their oar must be in every man's boat." They seem to have no business except to poke their noses into other people's business: they ought to have snub noses, for they are pretty sure to be snubbed.

Prying and spying, peddling and meddling, these folks are in everybody's way, like the old toll-gate. They come without being sent for, stop without being asked, and cannot be got rid of, unless you take them by the left leg and throw them down stairs, and if you do that they will limp up again, and hope they don't intrude. No one pays them, and yet they give advice more often than any lawyer; and though no one ever thanks them, yet there they are, peeping through keyholes and listening under the eaves. They are as great at asking questions as if they wanted you to say the catechism, and as eager to give their opinion as if you had gone down on your knees to ask it.

These folks are like dogs that fetch and carry; they run all over the place like starlings when they are feeding their young. They make much ado, but never do much, unless it is mischief, and at this they are as apt as jackdaws. If any man has such people for his acquaintances, he may well say, "save me from my friends."

> I know your assistance you'll lend,
> When I want it I'll speedily send;
> You need not be making such stir,
> But mind your own business, good sir.

It is of no more use than if we spoke to the pigs, for here is Paul Pry again. Paul and his cousins are most offensive people, but you cannot offend them if you try.

Well do I remember the words of a wise old Quaker: "John," said he, "be not concerned with that which concerns not thee." This taught me a lesson, and I made up my mind not to scrub other people's pigs for fear

I should soon want scrubbing myself. There is a woman in our village who finds fault with all, and all find fault with her; they say her teeth are all loose through her tongue rubbing against them; if she could but hold her tongue she would be happy enough, but that's the difficulty –

> "When hens fall a cackling take heed to the nest,
> When drabs fall a whispering farewell to thy rest."

Will Shepherd was sitting very quiet while others were running down their neighbours. At last a loose fellow sung out "Look at old Will, he is as silent as a stock-fish; is it because he is wise or because he is a fool?" "Well," said Will, "you may settle that question how you like, but I have been told that a fool cannot be silent." Will is set down as very odd, but he is generally even with them before he has done. One thing is sure, he cares very little what they do say so long as they don't worry his sheep. He hummed in my ear an old-fashioned verse or two the other evening, something like this –

> "Since folks will judge me every day,
> Let every man his judgment say;
> I will take it all as children's play,
> For I am as I am, whoever say nay.
>
> Many there be that take delight
> To judge a man's ways in envy and spite;
> But whether they judge me wrong or right,
> How the truth is I leave to you;
> Judge as ye list, whether false or true.
> Ye know no more than before ye knew,
> For I am as I am whatever ensue."

If folks will meddle with our business it is best to take no notice of them; there's no putting them out like letting them stop where they are; they are never so offended as when people neither offend them nor take offence at them. You might as soon stop all the frogs from croaking as quiet idle gossips when they once get on the chat. Stuff your ear with wool and let them jabber till their tongue lies still, because they have worn all the skin off of it. "Where no wood is the fire goeth out," and if you don't answer them they can't make a blaze for want of fuel. Treat them kindly, but don't give them the treat of quarrelling with them. Follow peace with all men, even if you cannot overtake it.

22
You can't catch the wind in a net.

Some people get windmills in their heads, and go in for all sorts of silly things. They talk of ruling the nation as if men were to be driven like sheep, and they prate of reforms and systems as if they could cut out a world of brown paper, with a pair of scissors. Such a body thinks himself very deep, but he is as shallow as a milk-pan. You can soon know him as well as if you had gone through him with a lighted candle, and yet you will not know a great deal after all. He has a great head, and very little in it. He can talk by the dozen, or the gross, and say nothing. When he is fussing and boasting of his fine doings you soon discover that he makes a long harvest of very little corn. His tongue is like a pig's tail, going all day long and nothing done.

This is the man who can pay off the National Debt, and yet, in his little shop, he sells two apples in three days: he has the secret of high farming, and loses more at it than any man in the county. The more he studies the more he misses the mark; he reminds me of a blind man on a blind horse, who rode out in the middle of a dark night, and the more he tried to keep out of ditches the more he fell in.

When they catch live red herrings on Newmarket heath he will bring out a good thing, and line his pockets with gold; up till now, he says, he has been unlucky, and he believes that if he were to make a man a coffin he would be sure not to die. He is going to be rich next year, and you will then see what you shall see: just now he would be glad of half-a-crown on account, for which he will give you a share in his invention for growing wheat without ploughing or sowing.

It is odd to see this wise man at times when his wits are all up in the moon: he is just like Chang, the Chinaman, who said, "Here's my umbrella, and here's my bundle, but *where am I*?" He cannot find his spectacles though he is looking through them; and when he is out riding on his own ass, he pulls up and says, "Wherever is that donkey?"

I have heard of one learned man who boiled his watch and stood looking at the egg, and another who forgot that he was to be married that day, and would have lost his lady if his friend had not fetched him out of his study. Think of that, my boy, and don't fret yourself because you are not so overdone with learning as to have forgotten your common sense.

The regular wind-catcher is soft as silk and as green as grass, and yet he thinks himself very long-headed; and so indeed he would be if his ears were taken into the measurement. He is going to do – well – there's no telling what. He is full of wishes but short of will, and so his buds never come to flowers or fruit. He is like a hen that lays eggs, and never sits on them long enough to hatch a single chick.

Moonshine is the article our friend deals in, and it is wonderful what he can see by it. He cries up his schemes, and it is said that he draws on his imagination for his facts. When he is in full swing with one of his notions, he does not stick at a trifle. Will Shepherd heard one of these gentry the other day telling how his new company would lead all the shareholders on to Tom Tiddler's ground to pick up gold and silver; and when all the talk was over, Will said to me, "That's a lie, with a lid on, and a brass handle to take hold of it." Rather sharp this of Will, for I do believe the man was caught on his own hook and believed in his own dreams; yet I did not like him, for he wanted us poor fellows to put our little savings into his hands, as if we could afford to fly kites with labourers' wages.

What a many good people there are who have religious crazes! They do nothing, but they have wonderful plans for doing everything in a jiffy. So many thousand people are to give half-a-crown each, and so many more a crown, and so many more a sovereign, and the meeting-house is to be built just so, and no how else. The mischief is that the thousands of people do not rush forward with their money, and the minister and a few hard-working friends have to get it together little by little in the old-fashioned style, while your wonderful schemer slinks out of the way and gives nothing. I have long ago found out that pretty things on paper had better be kept there. Our master's eldest son had a plan for growing plum-trees in our hedges as they do in Kent, but he never looked to see whether the soil would suit, and so he lost the trees which he put in, and there was an end of his damsons.

> "Circumstances alter cases;
> Different ways suit different places."

New brooms sweep clean, but they mostly sweep up dirt. Plough with what you please, I stick to the old horses which have served me so well. Fine schemes come to nothing; it is hard work that does it, whether it be in the world or in the church.

> "In the laborious husbandman you see
> What all true Christians are or ought to be."

23
Beware of the dog

John Ploughman did not in his first book weary his friends by preaching, but in this one he makes bold to try his hand at a sermon, and hopes he will be excused if it should prove to be only a ploughman's preachment.

If this were a regular sermon preached from a pulpit of course I should make it long and dismal, like a winter's night, for fear people should call me eccentric. As it is only meant to be read at home, I will make it short, though it will not be sweet, for I have not a sweet subject. The text is one which has a great deal of meaning in it, and is to be read on many a wall. "BEWARE OF THE DOG." You know what dogs are, and you know how you beware of them when a bull-dog flies at you to the full length of his chain; so the words don't want any clearing up.

It is very odd that the Bible never says a good word for dogs: I suppose the breed must have been bad in those eastern parts, or else, as our minister tells me, they were nearly wild, had no master in particular, and were left to prowl about half starved. No doubt a dog is very like a man, and becomes a sad dog when he has himself for a master. We are all the better for having somebody to look up to; and those who say they care for nobody and nobody cares for them are dogs of the worst breed, and, for a certain reason, are never likely to be drowned.

Dear friends, I shall have heads and tails like other parsons, and I am sure I have a right to them, for they are found in the subjects before us.

Firstly, let us *beware of a dirty dog* — or as the grand old Book calls them, "evil workers" — those who love filth and roll in it. Dirty dogs will spoil your clothes, and make you as foul as themselves. A man is known by his company; if you go with loose fellows your character will be tarred with the same brush as theirs. People can't be very nice in their distinctions; if they see a bird always flying with the crows, and feeding and nesting with them, they call it a crow, and ninety-nine times out of a hundred they are right. If you are fond of the kennel, and like to run with the hounds, you will never make the world believe that you are a pet lamb. Besides, bad company does a man real harm, for, as the old proverb has it, if you lie down with dogs you will get up with fleas.

You cannot keep too far off a man with the fever and a man of wicked life. If a lady in a fine dress sees a big dog come out of a horse-pond, and run about shaking himself dry, she is very particular to keep out of his way, and from this we may learn a lesson, - when we see a man half gone in liquor, sprinkling his dirty talk all around him, our best place is half-a-mile off at the least.

Secondly, *beware of all snarling dogs*. There are plenty of these about; they are generally very small creatures, but they more than make up for their size by their noise. They yap and snap without end. Dr. Watts said —

> "Let dogs delight to bark and bite,
> For God has made them so."

But I cannot make such an excuse for the two-legged dogs I am writing about, for their own vile tempers, and the devil together, have made them what they are. They find fault with anything and everything. When they dare they howl, and when they cannot do that they lie down and growl inwardly. Beware of these creatures. Make no friends with an angry man: as well make a bed of stinging nettles or wear a viper for a necklace. Perhaps the fellow is just now very fond of you, but beware of him, for he who barks at others today without a cause will one day howl at you for nothing. Don't offer him a kennel down your yard unless he will let you chain him up. When you see that a man has a bitter spirit, and gives nobody a good word, quietly walk away and keep out of his track if you can. Loaded guns and quick tempered people are dangerous pieces of furniture; they don't mean any hurt, but they are apt to go off and do mischief before you dream of it. Better go a mile out of your way than get into a fight; better sit down on a dozen tin-tacks with their points up than dispute with an angry neighbour.

Thirdly, *beware of fawning dogs*. They jump up upon you and leave the marks of their dirty paws. How they will lick your hand and fondle you as long as there are bones to be got: like the lover who said to the cook, "Leave you, dear girl? Never, while you have a shilling." Too much sugar in the talk should lead us to suspect that there is very little in the heart. The moment a man praises you to your face, mark him, for he is the very gentleman to rail at you behind your back. If a fellow takes the trouble to flatter he expects to be paid for it, and he calculates that he will get his wages out of the soft brains of those he tickles. When people stoop down it generally is to pick something up, and men don't stoop to flatter you unless they reckon upon getting something out of you. When you see too much politeness you may generally smell a rat if you give a good sniff. Young people need to be on the watch against crafty flatterers. Young women with pretty faces and a little money should especially *beware of puppies!*

Fourthly, *beware of a greedy dog*, or a man who never has enough. Grumbling is catching; one discontented man sets others complaining, and this is a bad state of mind to fall into. Folks who are greedy are not always honest, and if they see a chance they will put their spoon into their neighbour's porridge; why not into yours? See how cleverly they skin a flint; before long you will find them skinning you, and as you are not quite so used to it as the eels are, you had better give Mr. Skinner a wide berth. When a man boasts that he never gives anything away, you may read it as a caution – "beware of the dog." A liberal, kind-hearted friend helps you to keep down your selfishness, but a greedy grasper tempts you to put an extra button on your pocket. Hungry dogs will wolf down any quantity of meat, and then look out for more, and so will greedy men swallow farms and houses, and then smell around for something else. I am sick of the animals: I mean both the dogs and the men. Talking of nothing but gold, and how to make money, and how to save it – why one had better live with the hounds at once, and howl over your share of dead horse. The mischief a miserly wretch may do to a man's heart no tongue can tell; one might as well be bitten by a mad dog, for greediness is as bad a madness as a mortal can be tormented with. Keep out of the company of screw-drivers, tight-fists, hold-fasts, and blood-suckers: "beware of dogs."

Fifthly, *beware of a yelping dog*. Those who talk much tell a great many lies, and if you love truth you had better not love *them*. Those who talk much are likely enough to speak ill of their neighbours, and of yourself among the rest; and therefore, if you do not want to be town-talk, you will be wise to find other friends. Mr. Prate-apace will weary you out one day, and you will be wise to break off his acquaintance before it is made. Do not lodge in Clack Street, nor next door to the Gossip's Head. A lion's jaw is nothing compared to a tale-bearer's. If you have a dog which is always barking, and should chance to lose him, don't spend a penny in advertising for him. Few are the blessings which are poured upon dogs which howl all night and wake up honest householders, but even these can be better put up with than those incessant chatterers who never let a man's character rest either day or night.

Sixthly, *beware of a dog that worries the sheep.* Such get into our churches and cause a world of misery. Some have new doctrines as rotten as they are new; others have new plans, whims, and crotchets, and nothing will go right till these are tried; and there is a third sort, which are out of love with everybody and everything, and only come into the churches to see if they can make a row. Mark these, and keep clear of them. There are plenty of humble Christians who only want leave to be quiet and mind their own business, and these troublers are their plague. To hear the gospel, and to be helped to do good, is all that the most of our members want, but these worries come in with their "ologies" and puzzlements, and hard speeches, and cause sorrow upon sorrow. A good shepherd will soon fetch these dogs a crack of the head; but they will be at their work again if they see half a chance. What pleasure can they find in it? Surely they must have a touch of the wolf in their nature. At any rate, beware of the dog.

Seventhly, *beware of dogs who have returned to their vomit.* An apostate is like a leper. As a rule none are more bitter enemies of the cross than those who once professed to be followers of Jesus. He who can turn away from Christ is not a fit companion for any honest man. There are many abroad nowadays who have thrown off religion as easily as a ploughman puts off his jacket. It will be a terrible day for them when the heavens are on fire above them, and the world ablaze under their feet. If a man calls himself my friend, and leaves the ways of God, then his way and mine are different; he who is no friend to the good cause is no friend of mine.

Lastly, finally, and to finish up, *beware of a dog that has no master*. If a fellow makes free with the Bible, and the laws of his country, and common decency, it is time to make free to tell him we had rather have his room than his company. A certain set of wonderfully wise men are talking very big things, and putting their smutty fingers upon everything which their fathers thought to be good and holy. Poor fools, they are not half as clever as they think they are. Like hogs in a flower-garden, they are for rooting up everything; and some people are so frightened that they stand as if they were stuck, and hold up their hands in horror at the creatures. When the hogs have been in my master's garden, and I have had the big whip handy, I warrant you I have made a clearance, and I only wish I was a scholar, for I would lay about me among these free-thinking gentry, and make them squeal to a long metre tune. As John Ploughman has other fish to fry, and other tails to butter, he must leave these mischievous creatures, and finish his rough ramshackle sermon.

"Beware of the dog." Beware of all who will do you harm. Good company is to be had, why seek bad? It is said of heaven, "without are dogs." Let us make friends of those who can go inside of heaven, for there we hope to go ourselves. We shall go to our own company when we die; let it be such that we shall be glad to go to it.

24
Like cat like kit.

Most men are what their mothers made them. The father is away from home all day, and has not half the influence over the children that the mother has. The cow has most to do with the calf. If a ragged colt grows into a good horse, we know who it is that combed him. A mother is therefore a very responsible woman, even though she may be the poorest in the land, for the bad or the good of her boys and girls very much depends upon her. As is the gardener such is the garden, as is the wife such is the family. Samuel's mother made him a little coat every year, but she had done a deal for him before that: Samuel would not have been Samuel if Hannah had not been Hannah. We shall never see a better set of men till the mothers are better. We must have Sarahs and Rebekahs before we shall see Isaacs and Jacobs. Grace does not run in the blood, but we generally find that the Timothies have mothers of a godly sort.

Little children give their mother the headache, but if she lets them have their own way, when they grow up to be great children they will give her the heartache. Foolish fondness spoils many, and letting faults alone spoils more. Gardens that are never weeded will grow very little worth gathering; all watering and no hoeing will make a bad crop. A child may have too much of its mother's love, and in the long run it may turn out that it had too little. Soft-hearted mothers rear soft-headed children; they hurt them for life because they are afraid of hurting them when they are young. Coddle your children, and they will turn out noodles. You may sugar a child till everybody is sick of it. Boys' jackets need a little dusting every now and then, and girls' dresses are all the better for occasional trimming. Children without chastisement are fields without ploughing. The very best colts want breaking in. Not that we like severity; cruel mothers are not mothers, and those who are always flogging and fault-finding ought to be flogged themselves. There is reason in all things, as the madman said when he cut off his nose.

Good mothers are very dear to their children. There's no mother in the world like our own mother. My friend Sanders, from Glasgow, says, "The mither's breath is aye sweet." Every woman is a handsome woman to her own son. That man is not worth hanging who does not love his mother. When good women lead their little ones to the Saviour, the Lord Jesus blesses not only the children, but their mothers as well. Happy are they among women who see their sons and their daughters walking in the truth.

He who thinks it easy to bring up a family never had one of his own. A mother who trains her children aright had need be wiser than Solomon, for his son turned out a fool. Some children are perverse from their infancy; none are born perfect, but some have a double share of imperfections. Do what you will with some children, they don't improve. Wash a dog, comb a dog, still a dog is but a dog: trouble seems thrown away on some children. Such cases are meant to drive us to God, for he can turn blackamoors white, and cleanse out the leopard's spots. It is clear that whatever faults our children have, we are their parents, and we cannot find fault with the stock they came of. Wild geese do not lay tame eggs. That which is born of a hen will be sure to scratch in the dust. The child of a cat will hunt after mice. Every creature follows its kind. If we are black, we cannot blame our offspring if they are dark too. Let us do our best with them, and pray the Mighty Lord to put his hand to the work. Children of prayer will grow up to be children of praise; mothers who have wept before God for their sons, will one day sing a new song over them. Some colts often break the halter, and yet become quiet in harness. God can make those new whom we cannot mend, therefore let mothers never despair of their children as long as they live. Are they away from you across the sea? Remember, the Lord is there as well as here. Prodigals may wander, but they are never out of sight of the Great Father, even though they may be "a great way off."

Let mothers labour to make home the happiest place in the world. If they are always nagging and grumbling they will lose their hold of their children, and the boys will be tempted to spend their evenings away from home. Home is the best place for boys and men, and a good mother is the soul of home. The smile of a mother's face has enticed many into the right path, and the fear of bringing a tear into her eye has called off many a man from evil ways. The boy may have a heart of iron, but his mother can hold him like a magnet. The devil never reckons a man to be lost so long as he has a good mother alive. O woman, great is thy power! See to it that it be used for him who thought of his mother even in the agonies of death.

25
A horse which carries a halter
is soon caught.

With a few oats in a sieve the nag is tempted, and the groom soon catches him if he has his halter on; but the other horse, who has no rope dangling from his head, gives master Bob a sight of his heels, and away he scampers. To my mind, a man who drinks a glass or two, and goes now and then to the tap-room, is a horse with his bridle on, and stands a fair chance of being locked up in Sir John Barleycorn's stables, and made to carry Madame Drink and her habit. There's nothing like coming out fair and square, and standing free as the air. Plenty will saddle you if they can catch you; don't give them the ghost of a chance. A bird has not got away as long as there is even a thread tied to its leg.

> "I've taken the pledge and I will not falter;
> I'm out in the field and I carry no halter;
> I'm a lively nag that likes plenty of room,
> So I'm not going down to the 'Horse and Groom.'"

In other concerns it is much the same: you can't get out of a bad way without leaving it altogether, bag and baggage. Half-way will never pay. One thing or the other: be an out-and-outer, or else keep in altogether. Shut up the shop and quit the trade if it is a bad one: to close the front shutters and serve customers at the back door is a silly attempt to cheat the devil, and it will never answer. Such hide-and-seek behaviour shows that your conscience has just enough light for you to read your own condemnation by it. Mind what you are at, don't dodge like a rat.

I am always afraid of the tail end of a habit. A man who is always in debt will never be cured till he has paid the last sixpence. When a clock says "tick" once, it will say the same again unless it is quite stopped. Harry Higgins says he only owes for one week at the grocer's, and I am as sure as quarter-day that he will be over head and ears in debt before long. I tell him to clean off the old score and have done with it altogether. He says the tradespeople like to have him on their books, but I am quite sure no man in his senses dislikes ready money. I want him to give up the credit system, for if he does not he will need to outrun the constable.

Bad companions are to be left at once. There's no use in shilly-shallying; they must be told that we would sooner have their room than their company, and if they call again we must start them off with a flea in each ear. Somehow I can't get young fellows to come right out from the black lot; they think they can play with fire and not be burned. Scripture says, "Ye fools, when will ye be wise?"

> "April the first stands, mark'd by custom's rules,
> A day for being, and for making, fools;
> But, pray, what custom, or what rule, supplies
> A day for making, or for being, wise?"

Nobody wants to keep a little measles or a slight degree of fever. We all want to be quite quit of disease; and so let us try to be rid of every evil habit. What wrong would it be right for us to stick to? Don't let us tempt the devil to tempt us. If we give Satan an inch, he will take a mile. As long as we carry his halter he counts us among his nags. Off with the halter! May the grace of God set us wholly free. Does not Scripture say, "Come out from among them, and be ye separate, and touch not the unclean thing"?

26
An old fox is shy of a trap

The old fox knows the trap of old. You don't catch him so easily as you would a cub. He looks sharp at the sharp teeth, and seems to say,

"Hollo, my old chap,
I spy out your trap.

Today, will you fetch me?
Or wait till you catch me?"

The cat asked the mice to supper, but only the young ones would come to the feast, and they never went home again. "Will you walk into my parlour?" said the spider to the fly, and the silly creature did walk in, and was soon as dead as a door-nail.

What a many traps have been set for some of us. Man-traps and woman-traps; traps to catch us by the eye, by the ear, by the throat, and by the nose; traps for the head and traps for the heart; day traps, and night traps, and traps for any time you like. The baits are of all sorts, alive and dead, male and female, common and particular. We had need be wiser than foxes, or we shall soon hear the snap of the man-trap and feel its teeth.

Beware of beginnings: he who does not take the first wrong step will not take the second. Beware of drops, for the fellows who drink take nothing but a "drop of beer," or "a drop too much." Drop your drop of grog. Beware of him who says "Is it not a little one?" Little sins are the eggs of great sorrows. Beware of lips smeared with honey: see how many flies are caught with sweets. Beware of evil questions which raise needless doubts, and make it hard for a man to trust his Maker. Beware of a bad rich man who is very liberal to you; he will buy you first and sell you afterwards. Beware of a dressy young woman, without a mind or a heart; you may be in a net before you can say Jack Robinson.

"Pretty fools are no ways rare:
Wise men will of such beware."

Beware of the stone which you stumbled over the last time you went that way. Beware of the man who never bewares, and beware of the man whom God has marked. Beware of writing your name on the back of a bill, even though your friend tells you ten times over "It is only a matter of form, you know." It is a form which you had better "formally decline," as our schoolmaster says. If you want to be chopped up, put your hand to a bill; but if you want to be secure never stand as security for any living man, woman, child, youth, maiden, cousin, brother, uncle, or mother-in-law. Beware of trusting all your secrets with anybody but your wife. Beware of a man who will lie, a woman who tells tales out of school, a shop-keeper who sends in his bill twice, and a gentleman who will make your fortune if you will find him a few pounds. Beware of a mule's hind foot, a dog's tooth, and a woman's tongue. Last of all, beware of no man more than of yourself, and take heed in this matter many ways, especially as to your talk. Five words cost Zacharias forty weeks silence. Many are sorry they spoke, but few ever mourn that they held their tongue.

> "Who looks may leap, and save his shins from knocks;
> Who tries may trust, or foulest treachery find;
> He saves his steed who keeps him under locks;
> Who speaks with heed may boldly speak his mind.
>
> But he whose tongue before his wit doth run,
> Oft speaks too soon and grieves when he has done.
> Full oft loose speech hath bound men fast in pain,
> Beware of taking from thy tongue the rein."

27

A black hen lays a white egg.

The egg is white enough though the hen is black as a coal. This is a very simple thing, but it has pleased the simple mind of John Ploughman, and made him cheer up when things have gone hard with him. Out of evil comes good, through the great goodness of God. From threatening clouds we get refreshing showers; in dark mines men find bright jewels: and so from our worst troubles come our best blessings. The bitter cold sweetens the ground, and the rough winds fasten the roots of the old oaks. God sends us letters of love in envelopes with black borders. Many a time have I plucked sweet fruit from bramble bushes, and taken lovely roses from among prickly thorns. Trouble is to believing men and women like the sweetbriar in our hedges, and where it grows there is a delicious smell all around if the dew do but fall upon it from above.

Cheer up, mates, all will come right in the end. The darkest night will turn to a fair morning in due time. Only let us trust in God, and keep our heads above the waves of fear. When our hearts are right with God everything is right. Let us look for the silver which lines every cloud, and when we do not see it let us believe that it is there. We are all at school, and our great Teacher writes many a bright lesson on the black-board of affliction. Scant fare teaches us to live on heavenly bread, sickness bids us send off for the good Physician, loss of friends makes Jesus more precious, and even the sinking of our spirits brings us to live more entirely upon God. All things are working together for the good of those who love God, and even death itself will bring them their highest gain. Thus the black hen lays a white egg.

> "Since all that I meet shall work for my good,
> The bitter is sweet, the medicine is food;
> Though painful at present 'twill cease before long,
> And then, oh how pleasant the conqueror's song!"

28

He looks one way and pulls the other.

He faces the shore, but he is pulling for the ship: this is the way of those who row in boats, and also of a great many who never trust themselves on the water. The boatman is all right, but the hypocrite is all wrong, whatever rites he may practise. I cannot endure Mr. Facing-both-ways, yet he has swarms of cousins.

It is ill to be a saint without and a devil within, to be a servant of Christ before the world in order to serve the ends of self and the devil, while inwardly the heart hates all good things. There are good and bad of all classes, and hypocrites can be found among ploughmen as well as among parsons. It used to be so in the olden times, for I remember an old verse which draws out just such a character: the man says, -

> "I'll have a religion all of my own,
> Whether Papist or Protestant shall not be known;
> And if it proves troublesome I will have none."

In our Lord's day many followed him, but it was only for the loaves and fishes: they do say that some in our parish don't go quite so straight as the Jews did, for they go to the church for the loaves, and then go over to the Baptist chapel for the fishes. I don't want to judge, but I certainly do know some who, if they do not care much for faith, are always following after charity.

Better die than sell your soul to the highest bidder. Better be shut up in the workhouse than fatten upon hypocrisy. Whatever else we barter, let us never try to turn a penny by religion, for hypocrisy is the meanest vice a man can come to.

It is a base thing to call yourself Christ's horse and yet carry the devil's saddle. The worst kind of wolf is that which wears a sheep's skin. Jezebel was never so ugly as when she had finished painting her face. Above all things, then, brother labourers, let us be straight as an arrow, and true as a die, and never let us be time-servers, or turn-coats. Never let us carry two faces under one hat, nor blow hot and cold with the same breath.

29
Stick to it and do it.

Set a stout heart to a stiff hill, and the wagon will get to the top of it. There's nothing so hard but a harder thing will get through it; a strong job can be managed by a strong resolution. Have at it and have it. Stick to it and succeed. Till a thing is done men wonder that you think it can be done, and when you have done it they wonder it was never done before.

In my picture the wagon is drawn by two horses; but I would have every man who wants to make his way in life pull as if all depended on himself. Very little is done right when it is left to other people. The more hands to do work the less there is done. One man will carry two pails of water for himself; two men will only carry one pail between them, and three will come home with never a drop at all. A child with several mothers will die before it runs alone. Know your business and give your mind to it, and you will find a buttered loaf where a sluggard loses his last crust.

In these times it's no use being a farmer if you don't mean work. The days are gone by for gentlemen to make a fortune off of a farm by going out shooting half their time. If foreign wheats keep on coming in, farmers will soon learn that —

> "He who by the plough would thrive,
> Himself must either hold or drive."

Going to Australia is of no use to a man if he carries a set of lazy bones with him. There's a living to be got in old England at almost any trade if a fellow will give his mind to it. A man who works hard and has his health and strength is a great deal happier than my lord Tom Noddy, who does nothing and is always ailing. Do you know the old song of "The Nobleman's generous kindness"? You should hear our Will sing it. I recollect some of the verses. The first one gives a picture of the hard-working labourer with a large family

"Thus careful and constant, each morning he went,
Unto his day labour with joy and content;
So jocular and jolly he'd whistle and sing,
As blithe and as brisk as the birds in the spring."

The other lines are the ploughman's own story of how he spent his life, and I wish that all country-men could say the same.

"I reap and I mow, I harrow and I sow,
Sometimes a hedging and ditching I go;
No work comes amiss, for I thrash and I plough,
Thus my bread I do earn by the sweat of my brow.

"My wife she is willing to pull in a yoke,
We live like two lambs, nor each other provoke;
We both of us strive, like the labouring ant,
And do our endeavours to keep us from want.

"And when I come home from my labour at night,
To my wife and my children in whom I delight,
I see them come round me with prattling noise.
Now these are the riches a poor man enjoys.

"Though I am as weary as weary may be,
The youngest I commonly dance on my knee;
I find in content a continual feast,
And never repine at my lot in the least."

So, you see, the poor labourer may work hard and be happy all the same; and surely those who are in higher stations may do the like if they like.

He is a sorry dog who wants game and will not hunt for it: let us never lie down in idle despair, but follow on till we succeed.

Rome was not built in a day, nor much else, unless it be a dog-kennel. Things which cost no pains are slender gains. Where there has been little sweat there will be little sweet. Jonah's gourd came up in a night, but then it perished in a night. Light come, light go: that which flies in at one window will be likely to fly out at another. It's a very lean hare that hounds catch without running for it, and a sheep that is no trouble to shear has very little wool. For this reason a man who cannot push on against wind and weather stands a poor chance in this world.

Perseverance is the main thing in life. To hold on, and hold out to the end, is the chief matter. If the race could be won by a spurt, thousands would wear the blue ribbon; but they are short-winded, and pull up after the first gallop. They begin with flying, and end in crawling backwards. When it comes to collar work, many horses turn to jibbing. If the apples do not fall at the first shake of the tree your hasty folks are too lazy to fetch a ladder, and in too much of a hurry to wait till the fruit is ripe enough to fall of itself. The hasty man is as hot as fire at the outset, and as cold as ice at the end. He is like the Irishman's saucepan, which had many good points about it, but it had no bottom. He who cannot bear the burden and heat of the day is not worth his salt, much less his potatoes.

Before you begin a thing, make sure it is the right thing to do: ask Mr. Conscience about it. Do not try to do what is impossible: ask Common Sense. It is of no use to blow against a hurricane, or to fish for whales in a washing tub. Better give up a foolish plan than go on and burn your fingers with it: better bend your neck than knock your forehead. But when you have once made up your mind to go a certain road, don't let every molehill turn you out of the path. One stroke fells not an oak. Chop away, axe, you'll down with the tree at last! A bit of iron does not soften the moment you put it into the fire. Blow, smith! Put on more coals! Get it red-hot and hit hard with the hammer, and you will make a ploughshare yet. Steady does it. Hold on and you have it. Brag is a fine fellow at crying "Tally-ho!" but Perseverance brings home the brush.

We ought not to be put out of heart by difficulties: they are sent on purpose to try the stuff we are made of; and depend upon it they do us a world of good. There's a sound reason why there are bones in our meat and stones in our land. A world where everything was easy would be a nursery for babies, but not at all a fit place for men. Celery is not sweet till it has felt a frost, and men don't come to their perfection till disappointment has dropped a half-hundred weight or two on their toes. Who would know good horses if there were no heavy loads? If the clay was not stiff, my old Dapper and Violet would be thought no more of than Tomkins' donkey. Besides, to work hard for success makes us fit to bear it: we enjoy the bacon all the more because we have got an appetite by earning it. When prosperity pounces on a man like an eagle, it often throws him down. If we overtake the cart, it is a fine thing to get up and ride; but when it comes behind us at a tearing rate, it is very apt to knock us down and run over us, and when we are lifted into it we find our leg is broken, or our arm out of joint, and we cannot enjoy the ride. Work is always healthier for us than idleness; it is always better to wear out shoes than sheets. I sometimes think, when I put on my considering cap, that success in life is something like getting married: there's a very great deal of pleasure in the courting, and it is not a bad thing when it is a moderate time on the road. Therefore, young man, learn to wait, and work on. Don't throw away your rod, the fish will bite some time or other. The cat watches long at the hole, but catches the mouse at last. The spider mends her broken web, and the flies are taken before long. Stick to your calling, plod on, and be content; for, make sure, if you can undergo you shall *overcome*.

> If bad be your prospects, don't sit still and cry,
> But jump up, and say to yourself, "I WILL TRY".

Miracles will never cease! My neighbour, Simon Gripper, was taken generous about three months ago. The story is well worth telling. He saw a poor blind man, led by a little girl, playing on a fiddle. His heart was touched, for a wonder. He said to me, "Ploughman, lend me a penny, there's a good fellow." I fumbled in my pocket, and found two halfpence, and handed them to him. More fool I, for he will never pay me again. He gave the blind fiddler one of those halfpence, and kept the other, and I have not seen either Gripper or my penny since, nor shall I get the money back till the gate-post outside my garden grows Ribstone pippins. There's generosity for you! The old saying which is put at the top of this bit of my talk brought him into my mind, for he *sticks to it* most certainly: he lives as badly as a church mouse, and works as hard as if he was paid by the piece, and had twenty children to keep; but I would no more hold him up for an example than I would show a toad as a specimen of a pretty bird. While I talk to you young people about getting on, I don't want you to think that hoarding up money is real success; nor do I wish you to rise an inch above an honest ploughman's lot, if it cannot be done without being mean or wicked. The workhouse, prison as it is, is a world better than a mansion built by roguery and greed. If you cannot get on honestly, be satisfied not to get on. The blessing of God is riches enough for a wise man, and all the world is not enough for a fool. Old Gripper's notion of how to prosper has, I dare say, a good deal of truth in it, and the more's the pity. The Lord deliver us from such a prospering, I say. That old sinner has often hummed these lines into my ears when we have got into an argument, and very pretty lines they are *not*, certainly—

> "To win the prize in the world's great race
> A man should have a brazen face;
> An iron arm to give a stroke,
> And a heart as sturdy as an oak;
> Eyes like a cat, good in the dark,
> And teeth as piercing as a shark;
> Ears to hear the gentlest sound,
> Like moles that burrow in the ground;
> A mouth as close as patent locks,
> And stomach stronger than an ox;
> His tongue should be a razor-blade,
> His conscience India-rubber made;
> His blood as cold as polar ice,
> His hand as grasping as a vice.

His shoulders should be adequate
To bear a couple thousand weight;
His legs, like pillars, firm and strong,
To move the great machine along;
With supple knees to cringe and crawl,
And cloven feet placed under all."

It amounts to this: be a devil in order to be happy. Sell yourself outright to the old dragon, and he will give you the world and the glory thereof. But remember the question of the Old Book, "What shall it profit a man, if he gain the whole world, and lose his own soul?" There is another road to success besides this crooked, dirty, cut-throat lane. It is the King's highway, of which the same Book says: "Seek ye first the kingdom of God, and his righteousness; and all these things shall be added unto you." John Ploughman prays that all his readers may choose this way, and keep to it; yet even in that way we must use diligence, "for the kingdom of heaven suffereth violence, and the violent take it by force."

30

Don't put the cart before the horse.

Nobody will ever take that fellow to be a Solomon. He has no more sense than a sucking turkey; his wit will never kill him, but he may die for want of it. One would think that he does not know which side of himself goes first, or which end should be uppermost, for he is putting the cart before the horse. However, he is not the only fool in the world, for nowadays you can't shake your coat out of a window without dusting an idiot. You have to ask yourself what will be the next new piece of foolery.

Amusing blunders will happen. Down at our chapel we only have evening meetings on moonlight nights, for some of our friends would never find their way home down our Surrey lanes of a dark night. It is a long lane that has no turning, but ours have plenty of turnings, and are quite as long as one likes them when it is pitch dark, for the trees meet over your head and won't let a star peep through. What did our old clerk do the other Sunday but give notice that there would be no moon next Wednesday night in consequence of there being no service. He put the cart before the horse that time. So it was with the young parson, of very fine ideas, who tried to make us poor clod-hoppers see the wisdom of Providence in making the great rivers run near the large towns, while our village had a small brook to suit the size of it. We had a quiet laugh at the good man as we walked home through the corn, and we wondered why it never occurred to him that the Thames was in its bed long before London was up, and our tiny stream ran through its winding ways long before a cottager dipped his pail into it.

Dick Widgeon had a married daughter who brought her husband as pretty a baby as one might wish to see. When it was born, a neighbour asked the old man whether it was a boy or a girl. "Dear, dear," said Dick, "here's a kettle of fish! I'm either a grandfather or a grandmother, and I'm sure I don't know which." Dick says his mother was an Irishman, but I do not believe it.

All this is fun, but some of this blundering leads to mischief. Lazy fellows ruin their trade, and then say that bad trade ruined them.

Some fellows talk at random, as if they lived in a world turned upside down, for they always put things the wrong side up. A serving-man lost his situation through his drunken ways; and, as he could get no character, he charged his old master with being his ruin.

> "Robert complained the other day
> His master took his character away:
> 'I take your character,' said he, 'no fear,
> Not for a thousand pounds a year.'"

The man was his own downfall, and now he blames those who speak the truth about him. "He mistakes the effect for the cause," as our old schoolmaster says, and blames the bucket for the faults of the well.

The other day a fellow said to me, "Don't you think Jones is a lucky chap?" "No," said I, "I think he is a hard-working man, and gets on because he deserves it." "Ah," was the man's answer, "don't tell me; he has got a good trade, and a capital shop, and a fair capital, and I don't wonder that he makes money." Bless the man's heart; Jones began with nothing, in a little, poking shop, and all he has was scraped together by hard labour and careful saving. The shop would never have kept him if he had not kept the shop, and he would have had no trade if he had not been a good tradesman; but there, it's no use talking, some people will never allow that thrift and temperance lead to thriving and comfort, for this would condemn themselves. So to quiet their consciences they put the cart before the horse.

A very bad case of putting the cart before the horse is when a drinking old man talks as if he had been kept out of the grave by his beer, though that is the thing which carries people to their last home. He happens to have a strong constitution, and so he can stand the effects of drink better than most, and then folks say it was the drink which gave him the constitution. When an old soldier comes alive out of battle, do we think that the shot and shell saved his life? When we meet with a man who is so strong that he can be a great drinker and still seem little the worse, we must not say that he owes his strength to his beer, or we shall be putting the plough before the oxen.

When a man thinks that he is to make himself good before he comes to Jesus to be saved, he is planting the fruit instead of the root; and putting the chimney pots where the foundation should be. We do not save ourselves and then trust the Saviour; but when the Saviour has worked salvation in us, then we work it out with fear and trembling. Be sure, good reader, that you put faith first, and works afterwards; for, if not, you will put the cart before the horse.

31
A leaking tap is a great waster.

Aleaking tap is a great waster. Drop by drop, by
day and by night, the liquor runs away, and the
housewife wonders how so much can have gone. This is
the fashion in which many labouring men are kept poor:
they don't take care of the pence, and so they have no

pounds to put in the bank. You cannot fill the rain-water butt if you do not catch the drops. A sixpence here, and a shilling there, and his purse is empty before a man dares to look in it. What with waste in the kitchen, waste at table, and waste at the public-house, fools and their money soon part to meet no more. If the wife wastes too, there are two holes in the barrel. Sometimes the woman dresses in tawdry finery and gets in debt to the tally-man; and it is still worse if she takes to the bottle. When the goose drinks as deep as the gander, pots are soon empty, and the cupboard is bare. Then they talk about saving, like the man who locked the stable door after his horse was stolen. They will not save at the brim, but promise themselves and the pigs that they will do wonders when they get near the bottom. It is well to follow the good old rule—

> "Spend so as ye may
> Spend for many a day."

He who eats all the loaf at breakfast may whistle for his dinner, and get a dish of empties. If we do not save while we have it, we certainly shall not save after all is gone. There is no grace in waste. Economy is a duty; extravagance is a sin. The old Book saith, "He that hasteth to be rich shall not be innocent," and, depend upon it, he that hasteth to be poor is in much the same box. Stretch your legs according to the length of your blanket, and never spend all that you have:

> "Put a little by;
> Things may go awry."

It will help to keep you from anxious care, - which is sinful, if you take honest care, - which is commendable. Lay up when young, and you shall find when old; but do not this greedily or selfishly, or God may send a curse on your store. Money is not a comfort by itself, for they said in the olden time -

> "They who have money are troubled about it,
> And they who have none are troubled without it."

But though the dollar is not almighty, it ought to be used *for* the Almighty, and not wasted in wicked extravagance. Even a dog will hide up a bone which he does not want, and it is said of wolves that they gnaw not the bones till the morrow; but many of our working men are without thrift or forethought, and, like children, they will eat all the cake at once if they can. When a frost comes they are poor frozen-out gardeners, and ask for charity, when they ought to have laid up for a snowy day. I wonder they are not ashamed of themselves. Those are three capital lines—

> Earn all you can,
> Save all you can,
> Give all you can."

But our neighbour Scroggs acts on quite a different rule-of-three, and tries three other cans:

> "Eat all you can,
> Drink all you can,
> Spend all you can."

He can do more of all these than is canny; it would be a good thing if he and the beer-can were a good deal further apart.

I don't want any person to become a screw, or a hoarder, or a lover of money, but I do wish our working men would make better use of what they get. It is little enough, I know; but some make it less by squandering it. Solomon commends the good woman who "considereth a field and buyeth it: with the fruit of her hands she planteth a vineyard;" he also tells the sluggard to go to the ant, and see how she stores for winter. I am told that ants of this sort do not live in England, and I am afraid they don't; but my master says he has seen them in France, and I think it would be a good idea to bring over the breed. My old friend Tusser says,-

"Ill husbandry drinketh
Himself out of door;
Good husbandry thinketh
Of friend and of poor."

The more of such good husbandry the merrier for old England. You cannot burn your faggots in autumn and then stack them for the winter; if you want the calf to become a cow, you must not be in a hurry to eat neats' feet. Money once spent is like shot fired from a gun, you can never call it back. No matter how sorry you may be, the goldfinches are out of the cage, and they will not fly back for all your crying. If a fellow gets into debt it is worse still, for that is a ditch in which many find mud, but none catch fish. When all his sugar is gone, a man's friends are not often very sweet upon him. People who have nothing are very apt to be thought worth nothing: mind, *I* don't say so, but a good many do. Wrinkled purses make wrinkled faces. It has been said that they laugh most who have least to lose, and it may be so; but I am afraid that some of them laugh on the wrong side of their faces. Foolish spending buys a pennyworth of merry-making, but it costs many a pound of sorrow. The profligate sells his cow to buy a canary, and boils down a bullock to get half-a-pint of bad soup, and that he throws away as soon as he has tasted it. I should not care to spend all my living to buy a mouldy repentance, yet this is what many a prodigal has done, and many more will do.

My friend, keep money in thy purse: "It is one of Solomon's proverbs," said one; another answered that it was not there. "Then," said Kit Lancaster, "it might have been, and if Solomon had ever known the miss of a shilling he would have said it seven times over." I think that he does say as much as this in substance, if not in so many words, especially when he talks about the ant; but be that how it may, be sure of this, that a pound in the pocket is as good as a friend at court, and rather better; and if ever you live to want what you once wasted, it will fill you with woe enough to last you to your grave. He who put a pound of butter on a gridiron, not only lost his butter, but made such a blaze as he won't soon forget; foolish lavishness leads to dreadful wickedness, so John Ploughman begs all his mates to fight shy of it, and post off to the Post Office Savings' Bank.

> "For age and want save while you may;
> No morning's sun lasts all the day."

Money is not the chief thing, it is as far below the grace of God and faith in Christ as a ploughed field is below the stars; but still, godliness hath the promise of the life that now is as well as of that which is to come, and he who is wise enough to seek first the kingdom of God and his righteousness, should also be wise enough to use aright the other things which God is pleased to add unto him.

Somewhere or other I met with a set of mottoes about gold, which I copied out, and here they are: I don't know who first pricked them down, but like a great many of the things which are stuck together in my books, I found them here and there, and they are none of mine: at least, I cannot claim the freehold, but have them on copyhold, which is a fair tenure. If the owners of these odds and ends will call for them at the house where this book is published they may have them on paying a shilling for the paper they are done up in.

MOTTOES ABOUT GOLD.

A vain man's motto is............."Win gold and wear it."
A generous man's motto is..........."Win gold and share it."
A miserly man's motto is............"Win gold and spare it."
A profligate man's motto is........."Win gold and spend it."
A banker's motto is..................."Win gold and lend it."
A gambler's motto is................."Win gold or lose it."
A wise man's motto is................"Win gold and use it."

32
Fools set stools for wise men to stumble over.

This is what they call "a lark". Fools set stools for wise men to stumble over. To ask questions is as easy as kissing your hand; to answer them is hard as fattening a grey-hound. Any fool can throw a stone into a deep well, and the cleverest man in the parish may never be able to get it up again. Folly grows in all countries, and fools are all the world over, as he said who shod the goose. Silly people are pleased with their own nonsense, and think it rare fun to quiz their betters. To catch a wise man tripping is as good as bowling a fellow out at a cricket-match.

> "Folly is wise in her own eyes,
> Therefore she tries Wit to surprise."

There are difficulties in everything except in eating pancakes, and nobody ought to be expected to untie all the knots in a net, or to make that straight which God has made crooked. He is the greatest fool of all who pretends to explain everything, and says he will not believe what he cannot understand. There are bones in the meat, but am I to go hungry till I can eat them? Must I never enjoy a cherry till I find one without a stone? John Ploughman is not of that mind. He is under no call to doubt for he is not a doctor: when people try to puzzle him he tells them that those who made the lock had better make the key, and those who put the cow in the pound had better get her out. Then they get cross, and John only says – you need not be crusty, for you are none too much baked.

After all, what do we know if all our knowing was put together? It would all go in a thimble, and the girl's finger, too. A very small book would hold most men's learning, and every line would have a mistake in it. Why, then, should we spend our lives in perplexity, tumbling about like pigs in a sack, and wondering how we shall ever get out again? John knows enough to know that he does not know enough to explain all that he knows, and so he leaves the stools to the schools and the other – ools.

33

A man in a passion rides a horse
that runs away with him.

When passion has run away with a man, who knows where it will carry him? Once let a rider lose power over his horse, and he may go over hedge and ditch, and end with a tumble into the stone-quarry and a broken neck. No one can tell in cold blood what he may do when he gets angry; therefore it is best to run no risks. Those who feel their temper rising will be wise if they rise themselves and walk off to the pump. Let them fill their mouths with cold water, hold it there ten minutes at the least, and then go indoors and keep there till they feel cool as a cucumber. If you carry loose gunpowder in your pocket, you had better not go where sparks are flying; and if you are bothered with an irritable nature, you should move off when folks begin teasing you. Better keep out of a quarrel than fight your way through it.

Nothing is improved by anger unless it be the arch of a cat's back. A man with his back up is spoiling his figure. People look none the handsomer for being red in the face. It takes a great deal out of a man to get into a towering rage; it is almost as unhealthy as having a fit, and time has been when men have actually choked themselves with passion, and died on the spot. Whatever wrong I suffer, it cannot do me half so much hurt as being angry about it; for passion shortens life and poisons peace.

When once we give way to temper, temper will claim a right of way, and come in easier every time. He that will be in a pet for any little thing will soon be out at elbows about nothing at all. A thunderstorm curdles the milk, and so does a passion sour the heart and spoil the character.

He who is in a tantrum shuts his eyes and opens his mouth, and very soon says what he will be sorry for. Better bite your lips now than smart for life. It is easier to keep a bull out of a china shop than it is to get him out again; and, besides, there's no end of a bill to pay for damages.

A man burning with anger carries a murderer inside his waistcoat; the sooner he can cool down the better for himself and all around him. He will have to give an account for his feelings as well as for his words and actions, and that account will cost him many tears. It is a cruel thing to tease quick-tempered people, for, though it may be sport to you, it is death to them; at least, it is death to their peace, and may be something worse. We know who said, "Woe to that man by whom the offence cometh."

Shun a furious man as you would a mad dog, but do it kindly, or you may make him worse than he would be. Don't put a man out when you know he is out with himself. When his monkey is up be very careful, for he means mischief. A surly soul is sure to quarrel; he says the cat will break his heart, and the coal scuttle will be the death of him.

> "A man in a rage
> Needs a great iron cage.
> He'll tear and he'll dash
> Till he comes to a smash;
> So let's out of his way
> As quick as we may."

As we quietly move off let us pray for the angry person; for a man in a thorough passion is as sad a sight as to see a neighbour's house on fire and no water handy to put out the flames.

Let us wish the fellow on the runaway horse a soft ditch to tumble in, and sense enough never to get on the creature's back again.

34

Where the plough does not go, the weeds will grow.

In my young days farmers used to leave broad headlands; and, as there were plenty of good-for-nothing hedges and ditches, they raised a prime crop of weeds, and these used to sow the farm, and give a heap of trouble. Then

Farmer Numskull "never could make out nohow where all they there weeds could a come from." In those good old times, as stupids call them, old Tusser said:

> "Slack never thy weeding for dear or for cheap,
> The corn shall reward it when harvest ye reap."

He liked to see weeding done just after rain: no bad judge either. He said,

> "Then after a shower, to weeding a snatch,
> 'Tis more easy then the root to despatch."

Weeding is wanted now, for ill weeds grow apace, and the hoe must always go; but still lands are a fine sight cleaner than they used to be, for now farmers go a deal closer to work, and grub up the hedges and make large fields, to save every bit of land. Quite right, too. The less there is wasted the more there is for us all.

> To clothe the fields with plenty and all our barns endow,
> We'll turn up every corner and drive the useful plough.
> No weed shall haunt the furrow, before us all shall bow,
> We'll gaily yield our labour to guide the useful plough.

It would be well to do the same thing in other concerns. Depend upon it, weeds will come wherever you give them half a chance. When children have no school to go to they will pretty soon be up to mischief; and if they are not taught the gospel, the old enemy will soon teach them to thieve, and lie, and swear. You can tell with your eyes shut where there's a school and where there's none: only use your ears and hear the young ones talk.

So far goes the plough, and where that leaves off the docks and the thistles begin, as sure as dirt comes where there's no washing, and mice where there are no cats. They tell me that in London and other big towns vice and crime are sure to spread where there are no ragged schools and Sunday schools; and I don't wonder. I hope the day will never come when the good people will give up teaching the boys and girls. Keep that plough going, say I, till you have cut up all the charlock. Don't leave a rod of ground for the devil to sow his tares in. In my young time few people in our parish could either read or write, and what were they to do but gossip, and drink and fight, and play old gooseberry? Now that teaching is to be had, people will all be scholars, and, as they can buy a Testament for a penny, I hope they will search the Scriptures, and may God bless the word to the cleansing of their souls. When the schoolmaster gets to his work in downright earnest, I hope and trust there will be a wonderful clearance of weeds.

The best plough in all the world is the preaching of the gospel. Leave a village without Christ crucified, and it soon becomes a great tangle of thorn, and briar, and brake, and bramble; but when sound and sensible preaching comes, it tears all up like a steam plough, and the change is something to sing about. "The desert shall rejoice and blossom as the rose."

Inside a man's heart there is need of a thorough ploughing by God's grace, for if any part of our nature is left to itself, the weeds of sin will smother the soul. Every day we have need to be looked after, for follies grow in no time, and come to a great head before you can count twenty. God speed the plough.

35
All is lost that is poured into a cracked dish.

Cook is wasting her precious liquor, for it runs out almost as fast as it runs in. The sooner she stops that game the better. This makes me think of a good deal of preaching; it is labour in vain, because it does not stay in the minds of the hearers, but goes in at one ear and out at the other. When men go to market they are all alive to do a trade, but in a place of worship they are not more than half awake, and do not seem to care whether they profit or not by what they hear. I once heard a preacher say, "Half of you are asleep, half are inattentive, and the rest —." He never finished that sentence, for the people began to smile, and here and there one burst out laughing. Certainly, many only go to meeting to stare about.

> "Attend your church, the parson cries,
> To church each fair one goes;
> The old ones go to close their eyes,
> The young to eye their clothes."

You might as well preach to the stone images in the old church as to people who are asleep. Some old fellows come into our meeting, pitch into their corner, and settle themselves down for a quiet snooze as knowingly as if the pew was a sleeping-car on the railway. Still, all the sleeping at service is not the fault of the poor people, for some parsons put a lot of sleeping stuff into their sermons. Will Shepherd says they *mesmerize* the people. (I think that is the right word, but I'm not sure.) I saw a verse in a real live book by Mr. Cheales, the vicar of Brockham, a place which is handy to my home. I'll give it you:

> "The ladies praise our curate's eyes,
> I never see their light divine,
> For when he prays he closes them,
> And when he preaches closes mine."

Well, if curates are heavy in style, the people will soon be heavy in sleep. Even when hearers are awake many of them are forgetful. It is like pouring a jug of ale between the bars of a gridiron, to try and teach them good doctrine. Water on a duck's back does have some effect, but sermons by the hundred are as much lost upon many men's hearts as if they had been spoken to a kennel of hounds. Preaching to some fellows is like whipping the water or lashing the air. As well talk to a turnip, or whistle to a dead donkey, as preach to these dull ears. A year's sermons will not produce an hour's repentance till the grace of God comes in.

We have a good many hangers on who think that their duty to God consists in hearing sermons, and the best fruit of their hearing is to talk of what they have heard. How they do lay the law down when they get argifying about doctrines! Their religion all runs to ear and tongue: neither their heart nor their hand is a scrap the better. This is poor work, and will never pay the piper. The sermon which only gets as far as the ear is like a dinner eaten in a dream. It is ill to lie soaking in the gospel like a bit of coal in a milk-pan, never the whiter for it all.

What can be the good of being hearers only? It disappoints the poor preacher, and it brings no blessing to the man himself. Looking at a plum won't sweeten your mouth, staring at a coat won't cover your back, and lying on the bank won't catch the fish in the river. The cracked dish is never the better for all that is poured into it: it is like our forgetful heart, it wants to be taken away, and a new one put instead of it.

36
Grasp all and lose all.

While so many poor neighbours are around us it is a sin to hoard. If we do we shall be losers, for rats eat corn, rust cankers metal, and the curse of God spoils riches. A tight fist is apt to get the rheumatism, an open hand bears the palm. It is good to give a part to sweeten the rest. A great stack of hay is apt to heat and take fire; cut a piece out and let the air in, and the rest will be safe. What say you, Mr. Reader, to cut a few pounds out of your heap, and send them to help feed the orphans?

37
Scatter and increase.

People will not believe it, and yet it is true as the gospel, that giving leads to thriving. John Bunyan said,

> "There was a man, and some did count him mad,
> The more he gave away, the more he had."

He had an old saying to back him, one which is as old as the hills, and as good as gold –

> "Give and spend
> And God will send."

If a man cannot pay his debts he must not think of giving, for he has nothing of his own, and it is thieving to give away other people's property. Be just before you are generous. Don't give to Peter what is due to Paul. They used to say that "Give" is dead, and "Restore" is buried, but I do not believe it any more than I do another saying, "There are only two good men, one is dead, and the other is not born." No, no: there are many free hearts yet about, and John Ploughman knows a goodish few of them – people who don't cry, "Go next door," but who say, "Here's a little help, and we wish we could make it ten times as much." God has often a great share in a small house, and many a little man has a large heart.

Now, you will find that liberal people are happy people, and get more enjoyment out of what they have than folks of a churlish mind. Misers never rest till they are put to bed with a shovel: they often get so wretched that they would hang themselves only they grudge the expense of a rope. Generous souls are made happy by the happiness of others: the money they give to the poor buys them more pleasure than any other that they lay out.

I have seen men of means give coppers, and they have been coppery in everything. They carried on a tin-pot business, lived like beggars, and died like dogs. I have seen others give to the poor and to the cause of God by shovelfuls and they have had it back by barrow-loads.

They made good use of their stewardship, and the great Lord has trusted them with more, while the bells in their hearts have rung out merry peals when they have thought of widows who blessed them, and orphan children who smiled into their faces. Ah me, that there should be creatures in the shape of men whose souls are of no use except as salt to keep their bodies from rotting! Please let us forget them, for it makes me feel right down sick to think of their nasty ways. Let us see what we can do to scatter joy all around us, just as the sun throws his light on hill and dale. He that gives God his heart will not deny him his money. He will take a pleasure in giving, but he will not wish to be seen, nor will he expect to have a pound of honour for sixpence. He will look out for worthy objects; for giving to lazy, drunken spendthrifts is wasteful and wicked; you might as well sugar a brickbat and think to turn it into a pudding. A wise man will go to work in a sensible way, and will so give his money to the poor that he will be lending it to the Lord. No security can be better and no interest can be surer. The Bank is open at all hours. It is the best Savings' Bank in the nation. There is an office open at the Boys' and Girls' Orphanage, Stockwell, London. Draw your cheques or send your orders to C. H. Spurgeon. There will soon be five hundred mouths to fill and backs to cover. Take shares in this company. John Ploughman wishes he could do more for it.

38
Every bird likes its own nest.

It pleases me to see how fond the birds are of their little homes. No doubt each one thinks his own nest is the very best; and so it is for him, just as my home is the best palace for me, even for me King John, the king of the Cottage of Content. I will ask no more if providence only continues to give me —

> "A little field well tilled,
> A little house well filled,
> And a little wife well willed."

An Englishman's house is his castle, and the true Briton is always fond of the old roof-tree. Green grows the house-leek on the thatch, and sweet is the honey-suckle at the porch, and dear are the gilly-flowers in the front garden; but best of all is the good wife within, who keeps all as neat as a new pin. Frenchmen may live in their coffee-houses, but an Englishman's best life is seen at home.

> "My own house, though small,
> Is the best house of all."

When boys get tired of eating tarts, and maids have done with winning hearts, and lawyers cease to take their fees, and leaves leave off to grow on trees, then will John Ploughman cease to love his own dear home. John likes to hear some sweet voice sing —

> "Mid pleasures and palaces though we may roam,
> Be it ever so humble, there's no place like home;
> A charm from the sky seems to hallow us there,
> Which, wherever we rove, is not met with elsewhere.
>
> Home! Home! sweet, sweet home!
> There's no place like home!"

People who take no pleasure in their own homes are queer folks, and no better than they should be. Every dog is a lion at his own door, and a man should make most of those who make most of him. Women should be house-keepers and keep in the house. That man is to be pitied who has one of the Miss Gadabouts. Mrs. Cackle and her friend Mrs. Dressemout are enough to drive their husbands into the county jail for shelter: there can be no peace where such a piece of goods as either of them is to be found. Old Tusser said

"Ill huswifery pricketh
Herself up with pride:
Good huswifery tricketh
Her house as a bride.

"Ill huswifery moveth
With gossip to spend:
Good huswifery loveth
Her household to tend."

The woman whose husband wastes his evenings with low fellows at the beer-shop is as badly off as a slave; and when the Act of Parliament shuts up most of these ruin-houses, it will be an Act of Emancipation for her. Good husbands cannot have too much of their homes, and if their wives make their homes comfortable they will soon grow proud of them. When good fathers get among their children they are as merry as mice in malt. Our Joe Scroggs says he's tired of his house, and the house certainly looks tired of him, for it is all out of windows, and would get out of doors if it knew how. He will never be weary in well doing, for he never began. What a different fellow he would be if he could believe that the best side of the world is a man's own fireside. I know it is so, and so do many more.

"Seek home for rest,
For home is best."

What can it be that so deludes lots of people who ought to know better? They have sweet wives, and nice families, and comfortable houses, and they are several cuts above us poor country bumpkins, and yet they must be out of an evening. What is it for? Surely it can't be the company; for the society of the woman you love, who is the mother of your children, is worth all the companies that ever met together. I fear they are away soaking their clay, and washing all their wits away. If so, it is a great shame, and those who are guilty of it ought to be trounced. O that drink! that drink!

Dear, dear, what stuff people will pour into their insides! Even if I had to be poisoned I should like to know what I was swallowing. A cup of tea at home does people a sight more good than all the mixtures you get abroad. There's nothing like the best home-brewed, and there's no better mash-tub for making it in than the old-fashioned earthenware teapot. Our little children sing, "Please, father, come home," and John Ploughman joins with thousands of little children in that simple prayer which every man who is a man should be glad to answer. I like to see husband and wife longing to see each other.

> "An ear that waits to catch,
> A hand upon the latch;
> A step that hastens its sweet rest to win;
> A world of care without.
> A world of strife shut out,
> A world of love shut in."

Fellow workmen, try to let it be so with you and your wives. Come home, and bring your wages with you, and make yourselves happy by making everyone happy around you.

My printer jogs my elbow, and says, "That will do: I can't get any more in." Then, Mr. Passmore, I must pass over many things, but I cannot leave off without praising God for his goodness to me and mine, and all my brother ploughmen, for it is of his great mercy that he lets us live in this dear old country and loads us with so many benefits.

This bit of poetry shall be my finish: I mean every word of it. Let us sing it together.

> "What pleasant groves, what goodly fields!
> What fruitful hills and vales have we!
> How sweet an air our climate yields!
> How blest with flocks and herds we be!
> How milk and honey doth o'erflow!
> How clear and wholesome are our springs!
> How safe from ravenous beasts we go!
> And, oh, how free from poisonous things!
> "For these, and for our grass, our corn;
> For all that springs from blade or bough;
> For all those blessings that adorn,
> Both wood and field, this kingdom through;
> For all of these, thy praise we sing;
> And humbly, Lord, entreat thee too,
> That fruit to thee we forth may bring,
> As unto us thy creatures do."